THE AGE OF CALAMITY

TimeFrame AD 1300-1400

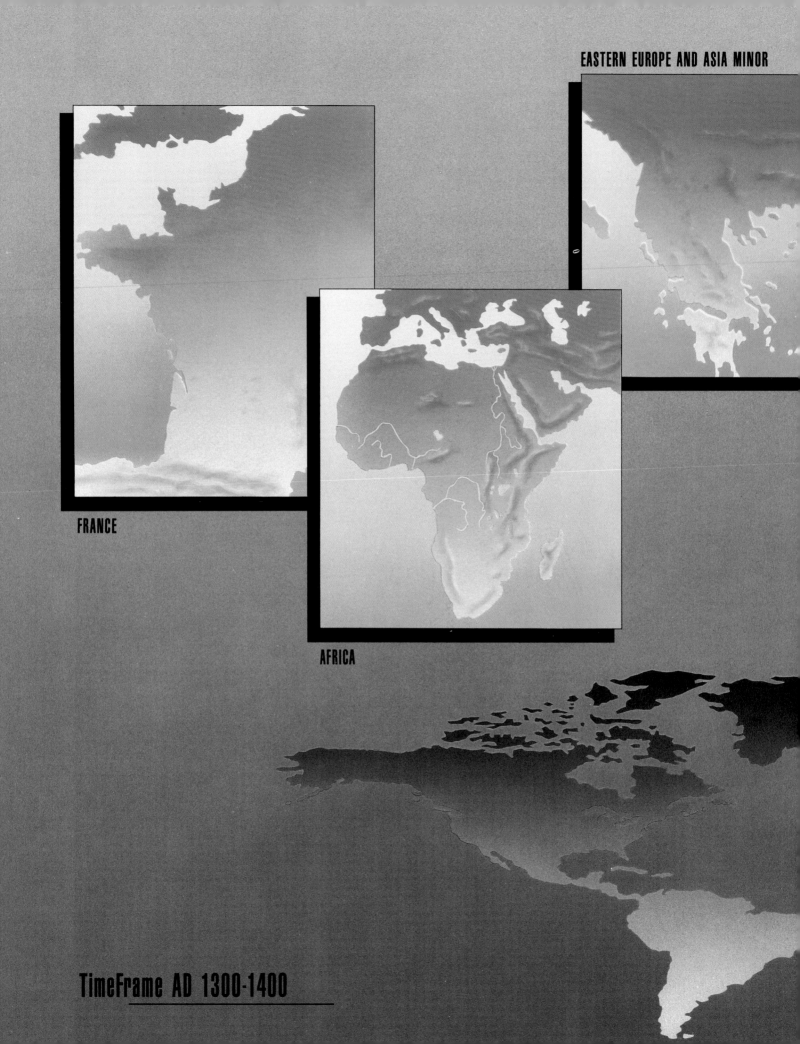

EASTERN EUROPE AND ASIA MINOR

FRANCE

AFRICA

TimeFrame AD 1300-1400

CHINA

CENTRAL ASIA

TIME® LIFE BOOKS

THE AGE OF CALAMITY

TimeFrame AD 1300-1400

BY THE EDITORS OF TIME-LIFE BOOKS

TIME-LIFE BOOKS, ALEXANDRIA, VIRGINIA

Time-Life Books Inc.
is a wholly owned subsidiary of
TIME INCORPORATED

FOUNDER: Henry R. Luce 1898-1967

Editor-in-Chief: Jason McManus
Chairman and Chief Executive Officer:
J. Richard Munro
President and Chief Operating Officer:
N. J. Nicholas, Jr.
Editorial Director: Richard B. Stolley
Executive Vice President, Books:
Kelso F. Sutton
Vice President, Books: Paul V.
McLaughlin

TIME-LIFE BOOKS INC.

EDITOR: George Constable
Executive Editor: Ellen Phillips
Director of Design: Louis Klein
Director of Editorial Resources:
Phyllis K. Wise
Editorial Board: Russell B. Adams, Jr.,
Dale M. Brown, Roberta Conlan,
Thomas H. Flaherty, Lee Hassig, Donia
Ann Steele, Rosalind Stubenberg
Director of Photography and Research:
John Conrad Weiser
Assistant Director of Editorial Resources:
Elise Ritter Gibson

EUROPEAN EXECUTIVE EDITOR:
Gillian Moore
Design Director: Ed Skyner
Assistant Design Director: Mary Staples
Chief of Research: Vanessa Kramer
Chief Sub-Editor: Ilse Gray

PRESIDENT: Christopher T. Linen
Chief Operating Officer: John M. Fahey, Jr.
Senior Vice Presidents: Robert M.
DeSena, James L. Mercer, Paul R.
Stewart
Vice Presidents: Stephen L. Bair, Ralph J.
Cuomo, Neal Goff, Stephen L. Goldstein,
Juanita T. James, Carol Kaplan, Susan J.
Maruyama, Robert H. Smith, Joseph J.
Ward
Director of Production Services:
Robert J. Passantino
Supervisor of Quality Control: James
King

Correspondents: Elisabeth Kraemer-Singh
(Bonn); Maria Vincenza Aloisi (Paris);
Ann Natanson (Rome). Valuable assis-
tance was also provided by Jane Walker
(Madrid); Felix Rosenthal (Moscow); Ann
Wise (Rome); Dick Berry (Tokyo).

TIME FRAME
(published in Britain as
TIME-LIFE HISTORY OF THE WORLD)

SERIES EDITOR: Tony Allan

Editorial Staff for *The Age of Calamity:*
Editor: Charles Boyle
Designer: Lynne Brown
Researchers: Caroline Alcock, Susie
Dawson
Sub-Editor: Christine Noble
Design Assistant: Rachel Gibson
Editorial Assistant: Molly Sutherland
Picture Department: Patricia Murray
(administrator), Amanda Hindley (picture
coordinator)

Editorial Production
Chief: Maureen Kelly
Production Assistant: Samantha Hill
Editorial Department: Theresa John,
Debra Lelliott

U.S. EDITION

Assistant Editor: Barbara Fairchild
Quarmby
Copy Coordinator: Colette Stockum
Picture Coordinator: Robert H.
Wooldridge, Jr.

Editorial Operations
Copy Chief: Diane Ullius
Production: Celia Beattie
Library: Louise D. Forstall

Special Contributors: Windsor Chorlton,
Stephen Downes, Ellen Galford, Robert
Irwin, Deborah Thompson (text); David
Nicolle, Stephen Rogers (research); Roy
Nanovic (index)

CONSULTANTS

General:
GEOFFREY PARKER, Professor of Histo-
ry, University of Illinois, Urbana-
Champaign, Illinois

C. A. BAYLY, Reader in Modern Indian
History, St. Catharine's College, Cambridge University, Cambridge, England

Western Europe:
CHRISTOPHER GIVEN-WILSON, Lectur-
er in Medieval History, University of St.
Andrews, Fife, Scotland

Eastern Europe and Asia Minor:
ROBERT IRWIN, Author of *The Middle
East in the Middle Ages*

Central Asia:
DAVID MORGAN, Lecturer in the Histo-
ry of the Near and the Middle East,
School of Oriental and African Studies,
University of London

China:
DENIS TWITCHETT, Gordon Wu Professor of Chinese Studies, Princeton University, Princeton, New Jersey

Africa:
BASIL DAVIDSON, Author of more than
thirty books on Africa, including *Africa
in History* and *Africa: History of a Continent*

**Library of Congress Cataloging in
Publication Data**

The Age of calamity: time frame AD 1300-
1400 / by the editors of Time-Life Books.
      p.   cm.—(Time frame series)
      Bibliography: p.
      Includes index.
ISBN 0-8094-6441-1.—ISBN 0-8094-6442-X
(lib. bdg.)
      1. Fourteenth century. 2. Disasters—History.
I. Time-Life Books. II. Series: Time frame.
D202.8.A38   1989
909'.2—dc19   89-4680
                                      CIP

Time-Life Books Inc. offers a wide range of fine
recordings, including a *Rock 'n' Roll Era* series.
For subscription information, call 1-800-621-
7026 or write Time-Life Music, P.O. Box C-
32068, Richmond, Virginia 23261-2068.

CONTENTS

THE MARCH OF THE BLACK DEATH

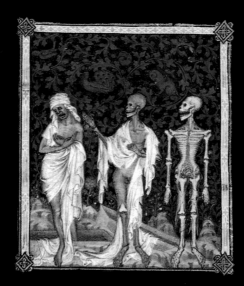

In the fourteenth century, divine retribution for the wickedness of humankind seemed to be the only possible explanation for the series of devastating blows under which the whole world reeled. In the first quarter of the century, Asia was afflicted by successive floods, earthquakes, famines, and droughts; in Europe, where since 1250 the climate had become colder and wetter, crops failed regularly and overcrowded communities suffered famine and disease. Worse was to follow. Out of the Far East came a sickness of unprecedented virulence that, between 1346 and 1352, carried off at least one-third of Europe's population. The greatest wave of mortality ever to sweep across the world, it was to become known as the Black Death.

The sickness struck in one of three forms, all caused by the bacterium *Pasteurella pestis*. Pneumonic plague attacked the lungs and septicemic plague the bloodstream. Bubonic plague, the third and commonest form, derived its name from the egg-size swellings—buboes—that appeared on the neck and in the armpits or groin during the early stages of the disease, to be followed by high fever and delirium. Those of stronger constitution might survive long enough to experience the excruciating bursting of the buboes. Usually, death offered the only relief from pain.

Sages blamed the spreading infection on movements of the planets, the putrefaction of the air by corpses, or the touching of infected bodies or clothes. It was even suggested that a mere glance from a sick person could be fatal. The real culprits, the black rats that infested most households of the time and whose fleas were contaminated with plague bacteria, would not be identified for centuries to come. When the rats died and the rodent population declined, the fleas turned to humans as suitable warm-blooded substitutes.

The terrible machinery of the plague appears to have been set in motion in the Gobi Desert in Mongolia. In the late 1320s, an epidemic erupted there among rodents and claimed its first human victims from within the ranks of the nomadic Mongol horsemen, who spread the disease throughout their extensive empire. The trade routes of the Silk Road, along which silks and furs were transported westward from China, exposed the whole of central Asia to the disease, and by 1345, Astrakhan on the Volga River and Caffa on the Black Sea had succumbed as infected fleas jumped from unpacked cargoes of furs.

The Black Sea marked the end of the overland trade routes from China and the beginning of the maritime ones to Europe. By late 1347, the rat-infested holds of Italian merchant ships had carried the pestilence to the ports of the Mediterranean, from which it quickly reached those of the French Atlantic coast. England paid dearly for its Bordeaux wines: Within a year, the Black Death was unwittingly imported along with the claret. By 1352, it had spread to Scandinavia, Germany, Poland, and finally Russia. In the few years since the disease had first entered Europe, its grim tour had claimed the lives of more than 20 million people.

The Italian writer Boccaccio, whose *Decameron* was cast as a collection of stories told by citizens in flight from the plague-ridden city of Florence, noted a variety of responses among the survivors. Some had no thought other than saving their own skins, their one purpose being "to flee from the sick and whatever belonged to them." Others sought oblivion in unbridled pleasure: "Day and night they went from one tavern to another, drinking and carousing unrestrainedly." A third, more moderate response was to continue life as normal but with the added precaution of carrying bouquets of fragrant flowers to "comfort the brain with such odors, especially since the air was oppressive and full of the stench of corruption, sickness, and medicines."

The doctors prescribed mysterious potions of herbs and other ingredients—including, for example, ten-year-old molasses and chopped-up snake—and lanced the swellings. If a physician tried bleeding a patient, he discovered that the plague victim's blood was thick and black and sometimes covered by a green scum. Only the priests were able to offer comfort: Confession, it was believed, would at least ensure an afterlife free from torment.

Far more efficacious were the preventive measures taken by a few determined communities. The despotic rulers of Milan walled up houses at the first sign of infection, imprisoning the sick and healthy together. The city of Nuremberg instituted a rigorous public-health program that involved the paving and cleaning of streets and the carting away of refuse. Personal cleanliness—for many, a completely new concept—was encouraged, and some workers even received bathing money as part of their wages. Milan and Nuremberg had possibly the lowest death tolls of the major European cities.

The devastation caused by the Black Death had passed its peak by the early 1350s, but there were further outbreaks in the following decades, and the plague persisted in Europe until the early eighteenth century. The massive decline in population transformed the relationship between people and resources. Since labor was scarce, the surviving work force could command high wages for their services, whereas the prices of land and agricultural products fell because of lack of demand. One English chronicler remarked: "A man could have a horse, which was worth forty shillings, for six shillings eight pence." Attempts to impose wage controls provoked widespread anger, and in England, the workers' heightened sense of their new economic importance contributed to the Peasants' Revolt of 1381. Similar uprisings occurred in other European countries.

Attitudes toward religion were changed as well. The clergy in general had shown as much human weakness as every other social group during the plague years, and they were now regarded as fallible and unjustifiably self-important. On the other hand, personal faith was strengthened as the frightening proximity of death focused people's minds on the afterlife. Cults of mysticism became popular, and in religious art, the image of death—often in the form of a ravenous skeleton leading the living to their graves—was a recurring motif. The deceased were depicted on their tombs as hideously emaciated and tortured, permanent witnesses to the social and psychological scars inflicted by the Black Death.

Spreading west from central Asia, the plague known as the Black Death was borne along land and maritime trade routes into the Middle East, North Africa, and Europe by infected fleas and rats that infested merchant cargoes. While some cities, such as Milan, were only lightly affected, many other communities were wiped out. In Europe alone, easily a third of the population succumbed. After cutting a deadly swath along the coasts of the Mediterranean and into Italy, France, and Spain, the course of the plague turned almost full circle, heading east again from northern Europe.

1351
1349
1349
1349
1352
1349
1349
1347
1348
1349
1348

Faster than graves can
dug for their interment
victims of the Black De
are carried to a cemet
hastily prepared outsid
the city walls of Tourn
Flemish textile town u
French protection, in
summer of 1349. This
lustration from the an
of the local abbot, Gil
Muisit, shows that the
dead of Tournai at lea
had the luxury of bein
buried in coffins. As th
ravages of the Black D
increased in intensity,
communities had to re
to removing corpses b
the cartload and buryi
them in mass graves. T
Italian writer Boccacci
reflecting in the years
followed, described ho
people became numb
the tragedy: "Nor for
their number were the
sequies honored by eit
tears or lights or crow
of mourners; rather, it
come to this, that a de
man was then of no m
account than a dead g
would be today."

Uniformed flagellants, whips poised above their shoulders, process behind the master of their society to whom they have sworn obedience. Before crowds of awed spectators in churches or market squares, the flagellants stripped to the waist and worked themselves into a frenzy by lashing their bodies with thongs of leather knotted with iron spikes. This self-scourging was an attempt to expiate the sins of humanity that, it was believed, had brought about the Black Death. The several hundred members of each society included both men and women, rich and poor; they were forbidden to wash, shave, or change their clothes, and the sexes were strictly segregated. Flagellism became prevalent in Germany in 1348, and at first was condoned by the Church, but the movement was banned in 1349 when the pope became concerned that their masters were claiming too much spiritual authority.

Christians look on with grim satisfaction as wood is added to the pyre in which Jews are being burned alive. Along with lepers and various racial or religious minorities, the Jews—deeply unpopular for their dealings in moneylending and dubbed the enemies of Christ by Church authorities—became scapegoats for the plague and were ruthlessly massacred throughout Europe. The most common accusation was that the Jews had deliberately contaminated public wells; the fact that they sustained as many casualties in the plague as the Christians did not influence popular prejudice or diminish the fervor of their most fanatical opponents, the flagellants. Pope Clement VI and certain other rulers condemned the massacres, but the persecution was pursued with vigor until 1351, by which time the Black Death was on the decline.

THE HUNDRED YEARS' WAR

1 In the dank depths of autumn, the gray swells of the English Channel promised an uneasy crossing between England and France. But if Henry Burghersh, bishop of Lincoln and councilor to the king of England, felt any queasiness on his voyage, it was more likely to be caused by the document in his possession than by the lurching of the deck underneath his feet. A few days earlier, on October 19, 1337, the royal councilors and their sovereign, Edward III, had met at the palace of Westminster to draft an angry message to Philip of Valois, king of France. Now, bearing the fruit of those deliberations, the bishop and his entourage disembarked and rode hard for the French capital at Paris.

At the Louvre, the royal palace of the French monarchy, the emissaries were received with scrupulous courtesy. The king took the parchment from the bishop's hand, perused it in silence, then passed it to a secretary to read aloud.

The letter consisted of two inflammatory statements. The first was Edward's assertion that he, not Philip, was the rightful king of France. Through his mother, Isabella, a French princess, Edward's claim to the crown was no less strong than Philip's own: Edward was the grandson of a French monarch, Philip of Valois a nephew. If Charles IV of France had not died without sons in 1328, Philip would never have reached the throne. This claim was not a new one; indeed, there were nobles in France who quietly supported it. But now the English monarch was prepared to back up his challenge by the use of force.

The second statement was equally provocative. Edward announced that, although he held vast tracts of land in France, he was no longer prepared to pay homage to the French king as his landlord. The fertile northern county of Ponthieu, as well as the wine-growing duchy of Aquitaine in the south, was his by hereditary right and by the grace of God alone, and he would rule these areas of France as freely as he ruled England. From this day forward, he declared himself to be the sworn enemy of the usurper, Philip of Valois.

A courtier who witnessed the delivery of this message reported that the king simply smiled at the bishop of Lincoln, complimented him on the skill with which he had carried out a difficult diplomatic mission, and told him that the letter did not require a reply. Philip then dismissed the delegates to their lodgings, sent them back to the coast with his personal guarantee of safe-conduct, and prepared for war.

The conflict that ensued would last far longer than the men who began it, and not even their grandsons would live to see its end. For 150 years the fight would go on, as a prolonged agony of sporadic skirmishes and uneasy truces punctuated by spells of intense and savage combat. Its effects would be felt far away from the battle-grounds, in fortunes lost and gained, in new patterns of government, in social up-heavals on an unprecedented scale. The conflict would become known to later ages

This manuscript illustration of the Battle of Poitiers, fought in 1356, shows King John II of France—mounted on a white charger and arrayed in a blue robe decorated with fleurs-de-lis—struggling in vain against the English. The engagement ended in defeat for the French; the king and many of his supporters were captured, leaving the country in a state of near anarchy. Recognizing their inability to match the English in the field of battle, the French knights retreated into castles and fortified towns, allowing the English to range freely over the countryside; in later campaigns of the long conflict that became known as the Hundred Years' War, they continued to avoid major encounters, choosing instead to wear down the English through skirmish and ambush.

as the Hundred Years' War, but those generations who lived and died in its shadow knew only that theirs was a time of perpetual strife.

In the volatile world of fourteenth-century European politics, challenges by rival claimants to a crown were not uncommon. Monarchs died without direct heirs; ruling families all over Europe were inextricably intermarried; customs varied from one land to another regarding the admissibility of female inheritors to a throne; the

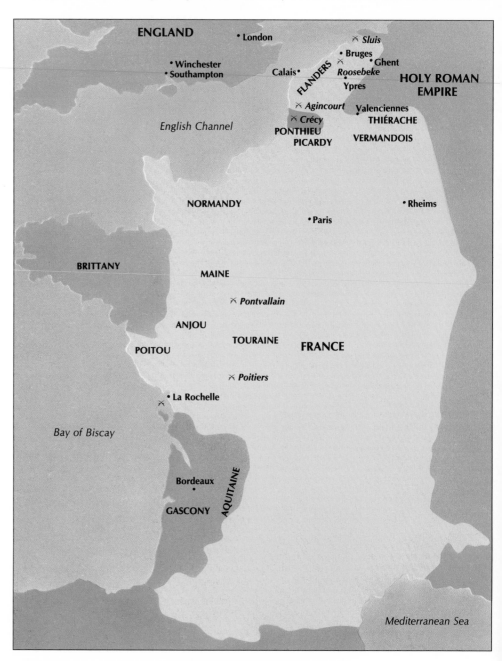

Disputes between Edward III—duke of Aquitaine and count of Ponthieu as well as king of England—and Philip VI of France concerning English territories in France *(orange area on the map)* were a decisive factor leading to the outbreak of the Hundred Years' War. Edward also claimed the French crown—he was a cousin of Philip VI—and had his royal coat of arms amended accordingly; the shield of his son, depicted in a stained-glass window in Saint Alban's Abbey *(above)*, shows the French fleur-de-lis combined with the lions of England. The English domains in France were considerably extended by the Treaty of Brétigny in 1360. Thereafter, however, the French gradually recovered most of the territory they had ceded, and by the 1370s, their fleet was raiding the south coast of England.

perils of childbirth were such that princes often outlived two or more wives and fathered multiple sets of descendants in the process. Edward's second challenge—his refusal to pay homage—was far more audacious, for it threatened the centuries-old set of social and property relationships that was later known as the feudal system.

At its simplest, the feudal bond was a link between a powerful person and a weaker one: In exchange for a vow of loyalty and military support, a king or noble would grant a lesser lord—the vassal—possession of a parcel of land that might, according to circumstance, be as small as a farm or as large as a province. Even a king could be a vassal to another king, if he held land that had been granted to him, or to his ancestors, within the other monarch's realm. The fourteenth-century Plantagenet kings of England were descendants of French princes and as such held territory in France as vassals of the French monarch; their ancestors included William, duke of Normandy, who had acquired the English crown by conquest in 1066.

Edward had become king of England in 1327, at the age of fourteen; Philip ascended the French throne in the following year. Soon thereafter, in accordance with feudal custom, Edward paid homage to his newly crowned kinsman for the lands he held in France. Now, in the letter dispatched to Philip in the care of the bishop of Lincoln, Edward had declared the feudal contract null and void.

But although the immediate political crisis was caused by Edward's repudiation of his allegiance to Philip of Valois, the issues raised went far beyond the breach of these bonds. Both monarchs were engaged in the lengthy process of asserting a central royal authority, and since the late thirteenth century, economic pressures, strategic considerations, and political strife had played their parts in generating and escalating the conflict between them. The French king had to contend with a tier of lords who were his vassals but, at the same time, enjoyed almost as much power as their sovereign: His great dukes and counts presided over their own courts and ruled their territories as semiautonomous states. The English king, as duke of Aquitaine and count of Ponthieu, was a French aristocrat and was obliged to defend the interests of his French overlord—but as king of England, Edward could hardly allow his French neighbor to dictate his foreign alliances or demand his support in wartime.

Three decades of negotiation had failed to solve the problem, which was complicated by economic links between England and France based on the vital commodities of salt, wool, and wine. England depended for its salt on the marshes of Brittany and Poitou, across the Channel; the weavers of the semiautonomous county of Flanders were the primary purchasers of pastoral England's vast output of wool; and Europe's thirst for good French wine could be quenched only by the cargoes passing through the English-held port of Bordeaux, where all the wines of Aquitaine were gathered, loaded, and taxed.

These economic concerns were inseparable from strategic considerations. It was vital to England to keep the wool, wine, and salt traffic moving freely, and it was equally crucial to France that it be able to control the sea traffic along its coasts. To guard against the possibility of French ports falling into enemy hands, Philip of France had begun to forge links with England's hostile neighbor, Scotland.

England and Scotland had been warring almost continuously since the 1290s. The Scots, led by their king, Robert Bruce, had repulsed a massive invasion force in 1314, subjecting Edward II's armies to a humiliating defeat at the Battle of Bannockburn. Although the third Edward had sealed a treaty with the Scots in 1328, soon after his own accession, he found it impossible to resist the temptation to intervene in their affairs; and after Bruce's death in 1329, he deposed the late ruler's young son, David II, and placed his own puppet on the disputed Scottish throne.

Philip was quick to give shelter to the exiled king. He sought to arbitrate between Scotland and England but insisted that no settlement was possible unless the exiled Bruce was reinstated. A sense of justice may have inspired his efforts on the young Scottish king's behalf, but the pleasure of seeing England under threat on two separate flanks was an equally strong incentive.

If Edward was rendered uneasy by the Franco-Scottish alliance, he was equally discomfited by the large fleet gathering in France's Channel ports. These vessels had originally been intended to take an army of European knights on a Crusade to the

Holy Land, but when the pope canceled the expedition, Philip moved his ships from the Mediterranean to the harbors of Normandy, virtually on England's doorstep. To Edward there could be only one explanation: The king of France was planning an attack on England, in support of the Scots. It was in these circumstances of mutual hostility and intimidation that Edward dispatched his challenge to Philip in 1337.

Each monarch prepared for the strife to come with the unshakable conviction that God was on his side. The thirteenth-century theologian Thomas Aquinas had set out the criteria for wars that could be launched with divine approval: just authority, just cause, and just intention. By just authority, he meant that only a prince or a monarch, invested with the divine mandate to defend his realm, had the authority to start a war and raise an army. To possess a just cause, the monarch had to make a stand against an evildoing enemy who merited the wrath that was about to be visited upon him. Finally, every participant in a just war had to be impelled by just intentions: Warriors had to be dedicated to the struggle against evil, not simply to personal gain.

If the royal combatants had not been prepared to turn a blind eye to this last condition, it would have been virtually impossible to recruit troops or allies, but lip service had to be given to the noble intentions of all who took up arms. And both protagonists believed in the righteousness of their cause: Edward III insisted that Philip denied him justice by withholding his legitimate inheritance in France; Philip's justification was his need to punish a rebellious vassal.

In terms of material resources, the French king appeared to have the advantage.

The broad, fertile kingdom of France, the wealthiest in Europe, boasted a population of some 21 million souls. Bounded on the northwest by the English Channel and extending southward to the Pyrenees, France was a land of powerful contrasts—of plains and mountains, cornfields and vineyards, cathedral cities and isolated hamlets, plateaus so densely populated that the church bells from one village rang clearly in the next, and barren wastes where a traveler might not meet another living person in the space of a full day's journey. Fully half the kingdom was governed directly by the king; the rest was under the control of his powerful vassals.

England was poorer. Its climate was less kindly than that of France, its population perhaps one-fourth the size of its neighbor's. Its capital, London, was barely half the size of Paris, and only a handful of towns, far smaller than their cross-channel counterparts, served as trade centers. Good farmland was concentrated mainly in the eastern counties and the midlands; the rest of the country was a landscape of moors, heaths, hills, and uncleared forest.

A miniature from a fourteenth-century manuscript, possibly Genoese, shows moneylenders counting coins *(left)*. Italian bankers helped finance both sides in the Hundred Years' War; the two greatest banking firms were bankrupted when Edward III of England failed to repay their loans. One of the main reasons for Italy's predominance in financial affairs was the stability of the gold currency of its major cities. Both France and England sought to learn from Italy's example. The French had gold coins of their own from the mid-thirteenth century; an écu dating from the reign of Charles VI is shown at right, above. Edward III minted the first English gold coins from 1344, one of which, showing the king in a ship *(right, below)*, commemorated an English naval victory at Sluis in 1340.

On both sides of the Channel, the same social structures predominated. A large rural peasantry—both free tenants and serfs bound to the soil they tilled—labored to provide the wealth of the land owned by their noble masters. Within this rural underclass, there were broad variations: peasants as prosperous as petty lords, homeless beggars, subsistence farmers for whom the weather's caprices spelled life or death. In the towns, a growing population of artisans, clerks, and merchants occupied society's middle ground.

French and English nobles, sprung from the same stock, shared the chivalric culture common to western Europe's upper classes. They practiced a common code of knightly conduct, observed the same niceties of courtly etiquette, and drew inspiration from the romances that celebrated the glorious deeds of Roland, King Arthur,

THE BATTLE FOR THE CHANNEL

The first great battle of the Hundred Years' War took place at sea. It happened on Midsummer Day 1340, off the port of Sluis in Flanders, where more than 200 ships had been assembled for a projected invasion of England. The English were outnumbered, but the longbows of their archers, stationed on specially built platforms at the rear of the ships, could fire arrows at a faster rate than the crossbows of the Genoese bowmen employed by the French.

Driven from the decks by the initial barrage of missiles, the soldiers crowding the French ships had no time to escape before the English fleet closed in. Grappling irons secured the French boats for boarding, and the rout was completed in fierce hand-to-hand fighting. Most of the French ships were sunk or captured.

The victory gave the English temporary control of the Channel and made it possible for them to land their forces unopposed anywhere along the French coast for the next twenty years.

Lancelot, and other legendary heroes. In both countries the nobility comprised two tiers: lesser lords, of small estates and fairly localized power, and a higher aristocracy consisting of a small but formidable elite—dukes, earls, counts, and viscounts, the princes of the realm. Here, however, the resemblance between the two kingdoms ended. The chief nobles of England were actively involved in the government of the entire realm; and although they might bear the titles of certain territories—Essex, for example, or Kent—they did not necessarily have jurisdiction over those lands. In France, the mighty dukes and counts were potentates in their own separate domains; unmoved by any embryonic sense of national identity, they did not automatically ally themselves with the king or concern themselves with the government of the realm.

The loyalty of his nobles was one of Edward's most conspicuous advantages, and he was able to secure the backing of Parliament—the assembly representing the nobility and the gentry—for raising taxes to fund the war effort. He was also able to use England's revenues from the wool trade as surety to raise loans from Europe's most important moneylenders, the great banking families of Italy. Nevertheless, the war would cause a serious drain on the Crown's resources: The cost of equipping, transporting, and maintaining an army on the far side of the Channel, and also of purchasing the goodwill of potential allies, would be astronomical.

Across the water, Philip found neither political nor financial support easy to come by. Lacking any central tax-raising facility, he had to appeal for funds to each locality in turn. Absorbed in the affairs of their own regions, the French nobility disputed the king's right to tax them and showed little inclination to provide the necessary financial or moral backing for the war. And Philip's domestic problems were aggravated by two major political disputes. Revolts in Flanders in 1338 had brought to power a local leader named Jacob van Artevelde; dependent on supplies of English wool to

maintain the weaving industries of Ypres, Ghent, and Bruges, the Flemish would soon acknowledge Edward as the rightful king of France. Farther south, the duchy of Brittany was enmeshed in a prolonged succession dispute, in which England fanned the flames by offering to back one faction in exchange for its support.

Both the exigencies of raising an army and the very nature of fourteenth-century warfare dictated a slow escalation. It was late in 1339, two years after Edward's challenge to Philip, before the first major campaign was launched.

In the decades that followed, both sides learned hard lessons about the art of warfare, and certain time-honored assumptions governing the conduct of battles were rendered obsolete. The struggle as a whole was a war of attrition, characterized less by the ritual engagements of jousting knights than by sieges and the raids and furtive attacks of guerrilla warfare. There were few pitched battles between massed armies. Most encounters were skirmishes between small armed bands contending for possession of a fortress or a strategic town, and much of the war was waged against civilians in the form of terrifying forays by irregular troops who pillaged and burned their way across the countryside, as well as long sieges against walled towns conducted for the express purpose of starving their inhabitants into submission.

The successful conduct of sieges was a tactical study in its own right. The first step was to cut off the defenders' water supply; then tunnels were dug under the walls and fires set in them, and burning projectiles were hurled over the battlements. Knowledge of gunpowder, invented in China in the ninth century, had recently reached Europe; first mentioned in a treatise dated 1327, cannon were to be employed by the English at the siege of Calais in 1346 and other engagements. Contemporary writers on the art of war recommended that captured defenders should not be killed but that they should be maimed, rendering them unable to fight or to work, and then sent home to burden ever-shrinking resources.

Medieval warfare was a predominantly seasonal occupation, best fought in the fall when all the reaping and sowing was done and when the hapless folk on the opposing side had harvested what they hoped would see them through the winter. Battles, too, were more easily won when the weather was

Sculpted in gilded bronze, an effigy showing Edward, "the Black Prince," son of Edward III of England, in full armor lies above his tomb in Canterbury Cathedral. Respected by friend and foe alike as the epitome of chivalric knighthood, he won his spurs at the Battle of Crécy in 1346 and ten years later captured France's King John at Poitiers. After being appointed prince of Aquitaine in 1362, however, he ruled over an extravagant court at Bordeaux and failed to win the loyalty of his French subjects. He returned to England in 1371, a sick and broken man. A year after his death in 1376, his only surviving son ascended the throne as Richard II.

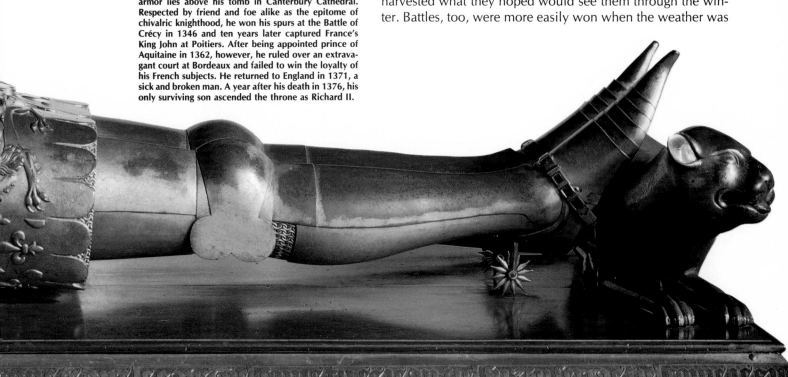

kinder and the troops not exhausted by the effort of keeping warm and dry.

On both sides of the Channel, men of all ranks were taught to see warfare as a way of life. Nobles were encouraged to practice their equestrian and martial skills in jousts and tournaments, and the lower orders were exhorted to train their sons in archery. At the start of the war, Edward issued an order forbidding peasants to play football or similar games, on pain of death; instead, they were to occupy their leisure hours practicing with bows and arrows. To make sure the populace had the necessary tools of the trade, the king canceled the debts of any artisan who made longbows.

Archers became an increasingly important part of any army in the field. If a native force did not possess enough men with this skill, there were mercenaries available for hire; most of the archers fighting on the French side were Genoese, adept at the use of the unwieldy crossbow. Other combatants in both the English and French armies—which usually numbered between 5,000 and 10,000 men—included common foot soldiers armed with swords, daggers, axes, and pikes, and lance-bearing warriors on foot or horseback. Each participant was required to supply his own weapons and armor; the knights who made up the cavalry also provided their own steeds. Equipping even the humblest fighting man became an ever more expensive business: It was estimated that the cost of providing weapons and protective clothing for an ordinary man-at-arms increased eightfold between 1300 and 1350.

But whatever the expenses of launching himself on a military career, a fighting man could look forward—provided he survived the war—to augmenting his fortunes. By the opening of the Hundred Years' War, the feudal obligation of military service that a vassal owed to his lord had been largely replaced by the employment of paid volunteers, who offered their services over a fixed term in return for wages and other financial incentives. They could hope to enrich themselves from sharing in the booty of plundered towns and from the ransom money paid for any captives taken. A garrison could command a fat fee from local civilians for defending their territory; a band of military marauders could extort a healthy sum from the nervous populace in exchange for a promise to leave them in peace. In theory, these perquisites were only supplementary to army pay; in fact, they often formed the largest part of a military income. Contemporary moralists lamented that war was no longer fought for glory but for gain. A new generation of professional warriors had been born.

With this soldiery at his disposal, Edward opened the first campaign of the war in 1339. Waiting until September, when the peasants of northern France had finished the harvest, he led an army of raiders on a five-week-long ride of terror—known in contemporary parlance as a *chevauchée*—laying waste to the districts of Cambresis, Vermandois, and Thiérache. In a letter to to his son and his royal councilors, Edward described these adventures: "On Monday, the eve of Saint Matthew, we left Valenciennes, and the same day the troops began burning in Cambresis, and they burned there through the following week, so that the country is clean laid waste, as of corn, cattle, and other goods. So we proceeded each day, our men together burning and destroying the country for twelve or fourteen leagues around."

As well as sowing terror, Edward expressly intended to seek out the French army and engage it in battle. But, although the two sides did eventually come face to face, Philip never gave his troops the command to fight. The result of this first campaign for England was thus a propaganda victory rather than a military one: The roads of the north were crammed with panic-stricken refugees. Learning of their plight, the pope sent 6,000 gold florins to Paris to help relieve their misery.

This late-fourteenth-century steel basinet—a close-fitting headpiece—is typical of a style of armored helmet that became increasingly common during the Hundred Years' War. The perforated cone-shaped visor deflected frontal blows, and the pointed rear gave a glancing surface when the head was tilted forward, as during a cavalry charge. The camail, a curtain of chain mail attached to the back, front, and sides, protected the wearer's neck and shoulders. The whole ensemble weighed about fifteen pounds. This helmet was probably made in northern Italy, the source of much of the armor used in France and England.

Throughout the war, this devastation of the countryside and its population was to cause severe damage to the French economy. But for the English also the costs of war were high, not least being that of transporting their troops and provisions across the Channel to France. Their commanders reckoned that chaos would ensue if soldiers were forced to live off a land that was being rapidly and systematically stripped of its food sources. To supply rations for the troops, the inhabitants of Southampton and Winchester were commanded to bake bread and brew beer in prodigious quantities. Beasts were assembled for slaughter near the Channel ports, and the mayor and aldermen of London sent out small cargo vessels to deliver fresh supplies at frequent intervals to the army in France.

The conveyance of war matériel was equally complicated. Tools and other equipment had to be brought along not only for fighting battles but for transporting baggage, setting up camp, and conducting sieges. One inventory of equipment shipped to France included—in addition to artillery pieces and other weapons—cranes, pulleys, winches, shovels, spades, mattocks, cutting tools, hammers, boxes filled with spare arrow shafts, horseshoes, horse collars, and harnesses, leather straps, baskets, chains, trestles, lanterns, assault ladders, small leather boats, and all the necessary components for assembling a floating bridge to span a river, canal, or moat.

England had no standing navy to transport its army and in times of crisis was compelled to draft merchant ships and other vessels into military service. But the importance of establishing control over the Channel became increasingly apparent to both sides, and when the inevitable clash at sea occurred on June 24, 1340, it proved to be the most decisive battle in the first phase of the war. The French, learning that Edward was planning to cross the Channel again, this time to Flanders, decided to launch a preemptive strike. Philip assembled an invasion force to be transported in his own vessels and those of his Genoese and Castilian allies. The two fleets met and fought just off the Flemish coast at Sluis, at the mouth of the Zwin River, the seaport of the rich cloth-weaving town of Bruges.

The English had the wind and the sun behind them and the tide in their favor; their greatest advantage, however, was the skill of their archers, plying their longbows from high platforms—known as castles—mounted on the decks of the ships. In force and fury, their volleys of arrows far outstripped the crossbow bolts fired off by the Genoese. In range, the crossbows could hit a target more than 1,600 feet away, whereas arrows shot from longbows rarely traveled as far as 1,000 feet; but crossbows were cumbersome, and even the most skilled practitioner could dispatch only two bolts per minute, in which time a master longbowman could fire off twelve arrows.

The English chronicler Geoffrey the Baker described how, as the ships from each side drew closer together, "an iron cloud of bolts fell upon the enemy, bringing death to thousands; then those who wished, or were daring enough, came to blows at close quarters with spears, pikes, and swords; stones, thrown from the ships' castles, also killed many." After hours of hard fighting, with massive losses on both sides, the French were defeated. Many of their soldiers, overwhelmed by the blizzard of arrows, were driven overboard. It was said that so much of their blood stained the sea that if the fishes had been given the power to speak, they would have done so in French.

By their victory at Sluis, the English decimated the French fleet and made themselves masters of the Channel. And despite occasional setbacks, the English were able to maintain their position during the next two decades. While the French were forced to rely on mercenary troops and foreign allies to field any kind of fighting force,

EUROPE'S FIRST ARTILLERY

The first recorded use of cannon in European warfare was during the siege of Calais between 1346 and 1347, when ten of the new weapons were deployed by the English. Early artillery pieces employed a charge of gunpowder, which was ignited through a touchhole *(inset)*, to fire either lead balls or arrow-shaped projectiles known as quarrels, as shown in the English manuscript illustration below; wadding wrapped around the shaft of the quarrel helped prevent the force of the explosion from dispersing.

Too unwieldy to be maneuvered on the battlefield, the cannon were used primarily to bombard bridges and gates; they remained ineffective against stone fortifications until larger weapons that could fire stone balls were developed during the following century.

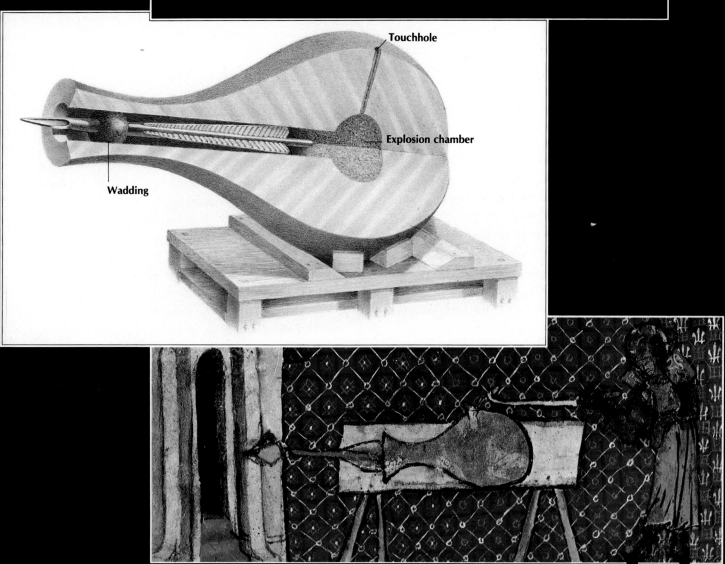

Touchhole

Explosion chamber

Wadding

Edward, enjoying the full support of his nobles, was able to make use of two or three virtually separate armies, each under the control of its own commander, operating singly on separate fronts or coming together to assault the French en masse. In 1346, the English defeated the Scots at the Battle of Neville's Cross near Durham, in which they captured the Scottish king. That same year, across the Channel in northern Picardy, about thirty miles from the coast, they won a decisive victory against the French at Crécy. Here, too, the longbowmen were the heroes of the day.

In theory, the French had all the advantages: Their army far outnumbered the

English, and they were meeting the enemy on their own home ground. Nevertheless, exhausted by a long march before the start of the battle, the French forces were plagued by ill luck and disorder once the armies met. A sudden rainstorm had soaked their Genoese archers' bowstrings, so that they lacked tautness; the English bowmen had kept their own strings dry by stowing them under their helmets. The English army took up its battle formation on a small piece of rising ground ideally suited for defense. The French, blinded by the sun, were overcome by a pincers movement of English archers; and as their cavalry tried to move forward against the barrage of arrows, their horses fell into concealed trenches. Those soldiers not crushed to death by their own side were hacked to pieces by English swords and spears.

The English followed up their victory at Crécy by seizing the Channel port of Calais after a long siege in 1347, but later that year, all conflict was brought to a halt by the arrival in Europe of the Black Death. The fatalities caused by this lethal strain of bubonic plague—some 20 million in just four years—set the casualty figures on both sides during the Hundred Years' War in a new and terrifying perspective, and for several years it seemed as if the survivors had been robbed of all resolve to continue. Peace negotiations were set in motion between Edward and John II, who succeeded his father as king of France in 1350; but in the end they could not come to terms, and the war resumed in 1355 when Edward dispatched two new armies to France.

One of these armies was led by Edward's soldier-son, the twenty-four-year-old Edward of Woodstock, known to later ages as the Black Prince because of the belief that he had worn black armor. He had enjoyed an early taste of blood and victory as a sixteen-year-old fledgling knight at Crécy; but the triumph that won him fame and popular adoration was the Battle of Poitiers in 1356.

Marching north through central France in an attempt to link up with the second English army, the Black Prince turned back toward Bordeaux when he learned that a much larger French force was pursuing him. The French caught up with him near Poitiers on September 17; however, John refrained from attacking the English on a Sunday and thus allowed the Black Prince to prepare his army for battle in marshy and wooded land unsuitable for cavalry. On the next day, the English longbowmen, firing from sheltered positions, again routed the mounted French knights. The fighting continued for eight hours, the English archers engaging the enemy in fierce hand-to-hand combat once their arrows had been spent, and the Black Prince's eventual victory was gloriously confirmed by the capture of the French king.

The triumphal return of the Black Prince to London, with John and many other noble captives in his train, was the occasion for an orgy of public rejoicing. The timbered houses were festooned with banners, the narrow streets carpeted with flowers, and so ecstatic were the crowds that it took several hours for the procession to travel the two miles from the city to the royal palace at Westminster.

Having captured the French king and humiliated the illustrious French knights at Poitiers, the English had good reason to believe that they could conclude the war on their own terms. But, in the absence of John II, his son Charles, the dauphin, managed to inspire the French with new determination: Encouraged by the pope's support for their cause, the dauphin's army forced the English to raise their siege of the city of Rheims and abandon hope of marching on Paris, and when representatives of both sides met for negotiations in 1360, the French were able to bargain from a position of some strength. The terms of the treaty drafted at Brétigny, a small settlement south of Paris, appeared to make massive concessions to the English, giving them full sovereignty over more than one-third of France. In exchange, however, Edward was expected to renounce his claim to the French throne and give up any notion of sovereignty in the areas outside those delineated in the treaty.

The agreement was partially ratified at Calais in the autumn of that year, but certain important clauses—regarding each king's renunciation of sovereignty over the other's newly agreed territories—were separated into another document, which was never sealed. As the new decade opened, overt hostilities had ceased, but the honor and ambitions of neither side were satisfied.

The peace between England and France was welcomed by no one more than the citizens of the French countryside. In Picardy, Normandy, Poitou, and other regions overrun by soldiery, great tracts of formerly fertile territory were reduced to wasteland and often remained in that state for decades, their inhabitants displaced, dispirited,

In an early-fourteenth-century manuscript illustration, armed rioters ransack the house of a wealthy Paris merchant. In both England and France, the urban poor and the rural peasants bore the brunt of taxes imposed to finance the war. The suffering of the needy was aggravated by poor harvests, rising prices, and the ravages of the Black Death, all of which contributed to sporadic rebellions throughout the century. A major uprising in France in 1358 known as the Jacquerie followed the French defeat at Poitiers in 1356. And in the English Peasants' Revolt of 1381, rebels sought an end to serfdom, but their pitchforks and homemade armor proved no match for the troops sent to suppress them.

or dead. The chronicler Jean de Venette grieved over the damage done to his native village in Beauvais after an English chevauchée in the 1350s: "No cock crowed, no hen called to her chicks. . . . The eye of man was no longer rejoiced by the accustomed sight of green pastures and fields covered by growing grain, but saddened by the nettles and thistles springing up on every side. The pleasant sound of bells was heard, indeed, not as a summons to divine worship, but as a warning of hostile incursions, in order that men might seek out hiding places before the enemy arrived."

As well as enduring organized raids by English troops, with their slash-and-burn tactics and systematic plunder, countrypeople suffered the depredations of armed companies of freelance warriors, dedicated to exploiting the state of chaos and extracting such profit as they could from a terrorized populace. These freebooters, running in packs, were known as *routiers;* the peasants generally called them "the English," although they were as likely to be Genoese, Castilian, or, indeed, French. Roaring into a district, they either stripped it bare or extorted protection money from its denizens in exchange for leaving them in peace.

Fields remained untilled, and food prices spiraled; the countryside was depopulated, if not by warfare then by famine and disease, as the Black Death continued the soldiery's grim work. Outside the castle walls of the nobility, their less privileged compatriots spoke bitterly of lords who made private bargains with the routier bands, and they even entertained their more presentable commanders at dinner while their underlings harried the cottage dwellers in neighboring villages.

Constant demands for taxes to pursue the war led to unrest and resentment: If the nobles of the realm refused to open their coffers, the king's officials had to turn their attentions to those lower down the social scale, imposing sales taxes on salt and staple foods, or manipulating the currency to debase the value of the scanty coins in the poor man's purse. Jean de Venette lamented the injustice—and the ineffectuality—of these measures in his memoir of the 1340s, when the fortunes of France had seemed at their lowest ebb: "In truth, the more money that was extorted in such ways in France, the poorer the king became. No prosperity in the kingdom ensued but, on the contrary, woe is me, every misfortune! Officials were being enriched, the king impoverished. Money was contributed to many nobles and knights that they might aid and defend their land and kingdom, but it was all spent for the useless practice of pleasures, such as dice and other unseemly games."

After the capture of the king at Poitiers, angry subjects castigated the upper classes: What had they done to aid the monarch, or rescue France, in the hour of need? In the towns, artisans and marketwomen mobbed and menaced the taxgatherers. In the battered countryside, a bloody rebellion—known as the Jacquerie, after the catchall nickname for a peasant, "Jacques Good-Man," or possibly after the short shirt, *jacques,* that was the characteristic garment of their class—set the poor against their masters. Inflamed with the stored-up wrath of generations, they raided castles and massacred their inhabitants, not sparing even babes in arms.

In 1358, an alliance of French nobles and neighboring princes abandoned their mutual rivalries to unite against this threat from below. The savagery with which they put down the uprisings in the countryside, and scoured the land to punish those who had dared raise a hand against their lords, was said to have exceeded the brutality of the routiers at their worst.

Some respite was afforded to the suffering peasantry by the nine-year peace that followed the Treaty of Brétigny in 1360. This precious breathing space also allowed the French time to reorganize their armies, put their finances in better order, and cement new political alliances. John II was released from captivity in London in 1360, when the French agreed to pay a ransom of £500,000 and send three of the king's sons as hostages to England; but when one of these sons broke parole, John—in an extreme chivalric gesture—voluntarily returned to London, where he died in 1364. The dauphin, now ruling as Charles V of France, initiated an energetic diplomatic campaign to win new friends and undermine the loyalty of England's disaffected supporters. Gradually, he unraveled the alliances that Edward had so painstakingly knitted together: The count of Flanders became more receptive to his influence, and even his dangerous eastern neighbor, the German emperor, began to look upon France more benignly.

When hostilities resumed in 1369, Charles V possessed not only a more efficient army and a well-filled war chest but—in the unlovely person of Bertrand du Guesclin, constable of France and supreme commander of the armies—a special military weapon. Even his most adulatory biographer could not deny that the Breton warrior was an uncouth and unprepossessing figure: "There was none so ugly from Rennes to Dinant. . . . Wherefore his parents hated him so sore that often in their hearts they wished him dead. Rascal, Fool, or Clown they were wont to call him; so despised was

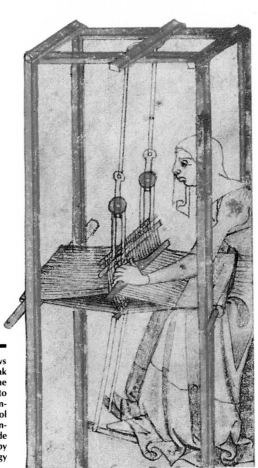

he as an ill-conditioned child that squires and servants made light of him." The son of impoverished minor nobles from Brittany, Guesclin had learned his military skills from the bottom up, as a fighter in the wars over the Breton ducal succession. His experience was that of a guerrilla rather than a champion in the jousts; when he needed information, and bribery failed, he would not scruple to resort to torture. Even his own side referred to him as "the hog in armor."

If his contemporaries were bemused by the rise of this rough diamond, Guesclin himself did not share their puzzlement: He was convinced that the configuration of the stars and planets, as well as a set of ancient prophecies ascribed to the magician Merlin, had predicted his triumphs. To ensure that he did not lose any of the opportunities that destiny afforded, Guesclin never did battle without consulting his staff astrologer. But in fact, there was nothing mystical about his achievements: He succeeded in shifting French tactics away from the pitched battles that had done them little good, and toward the ambushes and lightning raids that he understood so well.

Gradually, the tide of war began to

A fourteenth-century manuscript illustration shows cloth being woven on a floor loom. Before the outbreak of war, the mainstay of the English economy was the export of raw wool to Flanders, where it was made into cloth and sold throughout Europe, but heavy taxes imposed by the English kings on the export of raw wool caused a gradual decline in cloth manufacture in Flanders. The consequent transition in England to a trade based primarily on finished cloth was accelerated by the introduction of the fulling mill and other technology that increased output without raising labor costs.

turn in France's favor. In 1370, Guesclin defeated an invading English army at Pontvallain. Two years later, the Castilian fleet in alliance with the French destroyed the English fleet off La Rochelle. Victory bred optimism, and with the moral support of his nobles as well as their financial backing, Charles succeeded in recapturing nearly all the lands that had been given up to Edward in the Treaty of Brétigny. And the English were further weakened by severe political and economic problems.

At the start of the war, Edward III had managed his finances badly. He had run up huge debts, and his attempts to raise revenues by interfering with English wool traffic had thrown the trade into confusion and near disaster. During the years of English success, the war did, indeed, bring wealth into the kingdom, as soldiers of all ranks returned home with their spoils. But those who had remained at home were squeezed by ever-rising tax demands to subsidize the conflict. A popular song during the first years of the war complained that common folk were forced to sell their cattle, their dishes, and the clothes off their backs to meet the demands of the royal tax collectors.

To impose these taxes, the king needed the consent of Parliament. Originating in

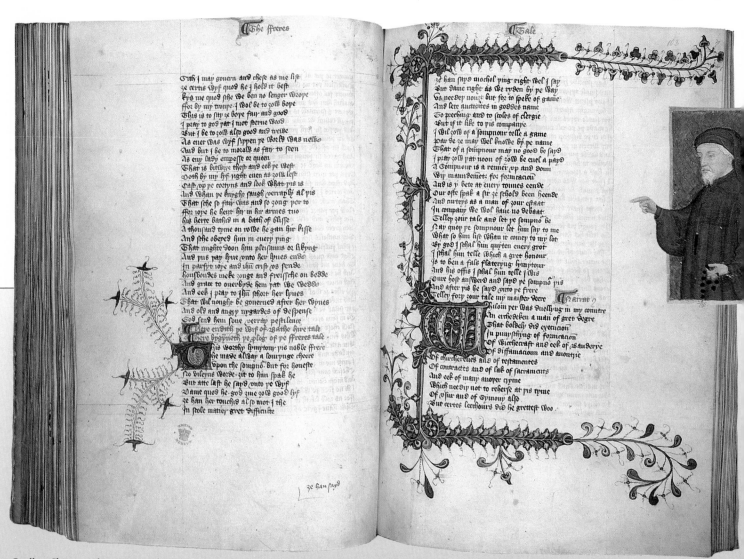

Geoffrey Chaucer points to a page from an early-fifteenth-century manuscript of his *Canterbury Tales*, a collection of stories told by a band of pilgrims.

the thirteenth century as an occasional and loosely structured forum extension of the royal council, Parliament had acquired its own rules, procedures, and statutory powers by the mid-fourteenth century. It comprised two main constituent groups: the Lords, numbering about 100 dukes, earls, and other high nobles as well as bishops and abbots; and the Commons, made up of knights—two from every shire in England—and burgesses, the leading citizens of all important towns, about 250 in all.

When Parliament assembled at Westminster in April 1376, the members of the Commons were angry. The country was in crisis. Overseas, the war was going badly; at home, financial chaos and high-level corruption went hand in hand. After meeting separately in secret session, the Commons confronted the Lords with their grievances. They complained of "numerous crimes and extortions committed by various people, and we have had no redress. Nor are there any persons about the king who will tell the truth, or give him loyal and profitable counsel, but they mock and they scoff, and they work always for their own profit. We declare to you therefore that we will do nothing further until those who are about the king, who are traitors and evil councilors, are dismissed from their offices, and until our lord king appoints as new members of his council, men who will not shirk from telling the truth, and who will carry out reforms."

So forceful was their case, and so real their power of withholding the right of taxation, that the Commons' demands were met: Corrupt advisers were impeached and removed from their positions, a new council was formed to advise the king, and for the time being, no new taxes were granted. From that day forward, the prestige and power of the Commons began to grow, and Parliament became the place where laws were made and the great affairs of state not only discussed but directed.

Two months after this assertion of political authority by the Commons, the Black Prince, who had returned to England from the duchy of Aquitaine in 1371 because of ill health, died of dysentery. The personification of a chivalric military tradition that was becoming rapidly outdated, he was mourned by friends and enemies alike and eulogized by the contemporary French chronicler Froissart as "the flower of the world's knighthood at that time and the most successful soldier of his age."

MASTERWORKS IN THE VERNACULAR

Dante writes in his study.

The dominant literary languages in Europe at the beginning of the fourteenth century were Latin, the universal language of the Church, and French, widely used in popular romances. But by the end of the century, writers in Italy and England had produced masterpieces in their native tongues, which gradually came to displace Latin as the vehicle of high art and contributed to a growing sense of national identity.

In Italy at the start of the century, an exiled Florentine named Dante Alighieri set out to create, in a language based on the dialect of Tuscany, an epic poem that could rival the classics of ancient Greece and Rome. The result was *The Divine Comedy*, which recounts the author's spiritual journey toward a revelation of divine glory.

Taking inspiration from Dante's followers Petrarch and Boccaccio as well as from French writers, the poet Geoffrey Chaucer forged in his *Canterbury Tales*—written between 1387 and 1400—a foundation for all subsequent English literature.

Born sometime in the 1330s in the independent county of Hainaut, close to the northern border of France, the chronicler Jean Froissart traveled widely throughout Europe and enjoyed the patronage both of the English royal court and of various noble families sympathetic to the French cause. Thus he was especially well qualified to compile an authoritative account of the great events of his generation, and in particular of the longstanding rivalry between the two nations.

Froissart reported information gathered from eyewitness sources on both sides in a dramatic narrative enlivened with reconstructed dialogue and lavish descriptions of weddings and funerals, which he included to satisfy the taste of his aristocratic patrons. Froissart's descriptions of the battles of the Hundred Years' War are so vivid that he has been described as the world's first great journalist.

The page reproduced at right, taken from a fifteenth-century manuscript edition of Froissart's *Chronicles*, shows the ceremonial entry of Isabelle of Bavaria, wife of Charles VI of France, into Paris in 1389.

CHRONICLER OF AN AGE

His father did not long survive him. In 1377, a year after celebrating the jubilee that marked his half-century on the throne, Edward III was buried at Westminster. His successor was his ten-year-old grandchild, Richard, son of the Black Prince. After years of enjoying the upper hand, England now found itself on the defensive—defeated in France, its southern coast raided by enemy ships, and governed by a child-king who was surrounded by nobles jockeying for control. Nor were the ambitious nobles the new king's only dissatisfied subjects. In June 1381, England experienced its own popular uprisings when, following decades of suffering caused by oppressive taxation and the ravages of the Black Death, an army of angry peasants and urban poor rose up in the counties of Essex and Kent and marched on London. Brandishing axes, scythes, longbows, and battered swords, they had been roused to fury by the latest tax demand: a poll tax, the third in four years, to be imposed on every subject over the age of fifteen. They had seen how easily the rich were able to bribe the taxgatherers to forget or miscount their households, and how readily corrupt officials lined their own pockets at the expense of the poor.

But the peasants' grievances went beyond the subject of taxation: They demanded an end to serfdom. They were fired by the egalitarian speeches of their mentor, the priest John Ball: "Are we not all descended from the same parents, Adam and Eve?" he asked, and looked forward to the day when "all things shall be held in common; when there shall be neither vassals nor lords, when the lords shall be no more masters than ourselves." No longer prepared to pay rent to their landlords in the form of compulsory labor, the peasants demanded the right to pay a fixed rent for the ground they tilled. On their march, they forced open the prisons, burned public records, and ransacked the houses of the rich. The zealots among them hunted down the officials and landlords who had most oppressed them and stuck their severed heads on poles.

Bearing these grisly standards, some 10,000 angry peasants set up camp outside the walls of London and demanded an audience with the king. Surrounded by a company of knights, the young Richard II listened to the stream of demands, then commanded a party of clerks to begin writing out charters on the spot. Some peasants, believing their cause to be won, turned away and headed home; but their more cynical leader, the fiery Wat Tyler, disbelieved the king's promises and urged his followers to hold fast. He demanded a confrontation with the king; while he was pressing his demands, he was stabbed to death by the mayor of London. Thrown into confusion, his followers were routed and the revolt suppressed.

France, too, was distracted from war by domestic rebellion. In the late 1370s, the merchant-citizens of the commercial cities of Ghent and Bruges rose in revolt against the count of Flanders. Their leader, Philip van Artevelde—the son of Jacob, who had led the rebellion of 1338—sought to unite the whole of Flanders in a battle for independence, in which not only the count of Flanders but the king of France would be driven out of the land. He held out the hope of a commonwealth of equals: "When we hold a conference," he promised his followers, "everyone can come and give counsel, the poor as well as the rich." He sought aid from the English, trusting them to be ready allies for any venture that would discomfit the French king; but before he had received anything more than verbal support, he learned that the armies of the king and nobles of France were on the march against him.

Summoning every able-bodied man in the vicinity of Ghent, where his power base was strongest, he marshaled his own army. Wearing caps of iron and wielding bludgeons, knives, and iron-tipped staves, Philip's rebels marched under the banners

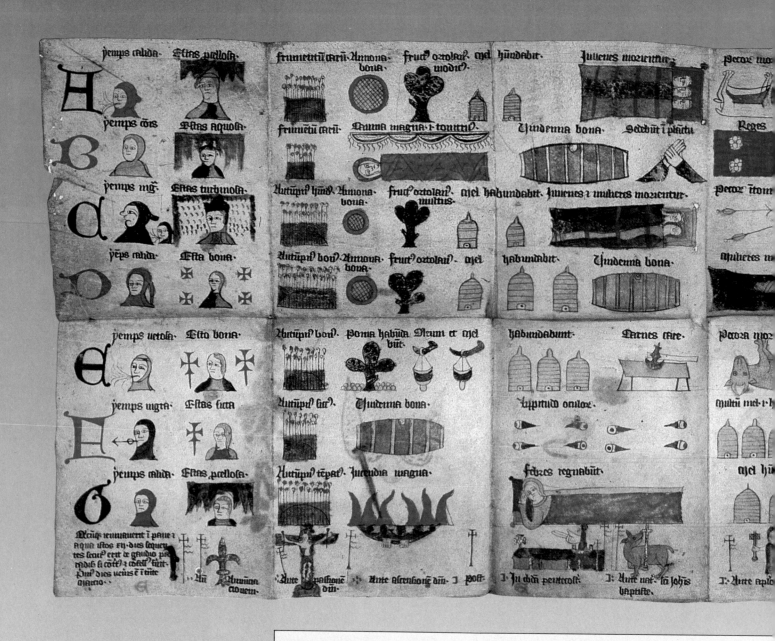

In fourteenth-century Europe, the influence of the planets on the affairs of the world was perceived as second only to that of God. The rediscovery of classical learning in the twelfth and thirteenth centuries had restored to western Europe the study of astrology, for centuries past a specialty of the Islamic world, and the practice of divining future events from the configuration of the heavenly bodies became a respected field of research.

The connection between astrology and medicine, one of the few sciences that was not permeated by Christian doctrines, was especially strong; in one instance, the physicians of the medical faculty at the University of Paris reported to King Philip VI that the terrible affliction of the Black Death was a direct result of the triple conjunction of the planets Saturn, Mars, and Jupiter in the house of Aquarius on the 20th of March in 1345. Chairs of astrology were

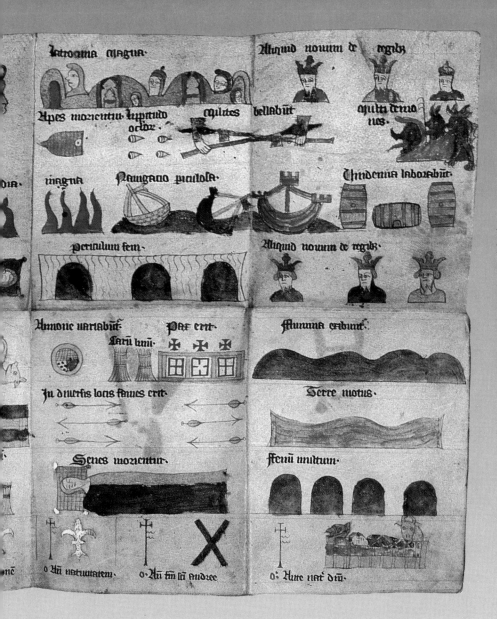

established at universities in France and Italy, and rulers such as King Charles V of France commissioned translations of astrological treatises.

In addition to these highly regarded scholarly works, pocket-size popular versions of almanacs were read throughout Europe. Typically, the volumes consisted of an almanac proper, which listed the astronomical events of the upcoming year, a calendar of the ecclesiastical year, as well as

A CHART OF THE FUTURE

an astrological forecast of notable events.

The section from a well-thumbed English example shown here contains predictions for seven years, each labeled with a letter and illustrated with a row of pictographs captioned in Latin. An explanation of some of the symbols is given at right above.

This life-size portrait of Richard II of England was commissioned by the king in the early 1390s and was placed at the back of his pew in the choir of Westminster Abbey to symbolize the ruler's perpetual spiritual presence in the church. Despite the rigid, conventional pose, the unknown painter took care to render the face with vivid naturalistic detail, making the portrait one of the first genuine likenesses of an English monarch.

of their towns and trade guilds to meet the royal forces at the Flemish town of Roosebeke in 1382. The battle took place in bitter November weather, and although the rebels made a strong stand, they were eventually routed by the superior weaponry and tactics of the foe. In the course of his troops' headlong retreat, van Artevelde was trampled to death. After the battle, the duke of Burgundy commissioned a carpet woven with van Artevelde's likeness, to allow himself the daily satisfaction of treading on the face of this audacious challenger to the social order.

In 1380, on the death of his father, Charles VI succeeded to the French throne at the age of twelve. Both France and England were now ruled by boy-kings. Guesclin, the French champion, had died in the same year as his royal master. On both sides of the Channel, men were weary of the war, and in 1384, negotiations for peace began in earnest. These were not the first attempts at settlement—there had been overtures and parleys ever since the war began—but, despite mutual mistrust, it seemed to England and France that the time had come to negotiate a lasting peace.

The site chosen for the discussions was the battle-scarred hamlet of Leulinghen, on the banks of the Somme River. Neither side possessed permanent ambassadors; the formal heads of each delegation, with royal authority to conclude treaties, were members of the high nobility—the dukes of Burgundy and Berry leading the French, the dukes of Lancaster and Gloucester acting for the English king. The real work, however, was done by a battery of legal experts—senior clerics, royal councilors, men of letters—and the logistics of bringing these parties together were almost as complex as the peace negotiations themselves. When the great dukes finally made their appearance, each brought an entourage of at least 500 followers. A vast city of tents was erected to house these peace-seeking armies; the most prominent among them was the magnificent canvas palace of the duke of Burgundy, cunningly painted with portcullis and battlements.

Both parties were more than willing to make concessions, and a spirit of optimism prevailed. But the old issue of sovereignty remained a sticking point: The French were ready to give up considerable amounts of territory, as long as the English paid homage to the French king for these lands. The English in turn demanded complete sovereignty, or nothing. Financial obstacles stood between the two as well: The English insisted on payment of French arrears for their late king's ransom; the French claimed massive reparations for war damages. The meetings at Leulinghen went on for more than a decade without any agreement on these issues.

In 1395, desperate for a solution, the negotiators reckoned that a long-term truce might, in effect, put a stop to the war, especially if it could be cemented by a diplomatic marriage. The alliance they had in mind would bind the two rival monarchies together: Richard II, now aged twenty-eight, would make an ideal husband for Isabelle, the daughter of Charles VI of France. The fact that the bride was no more than seven years old did not deter the matchmakers. The groom was willing; indeed, the proposal of marriage had allegedly been his idea.

The ceremony of reconciliation between the kings took place in October 1396, on the outskirts of Calais, in a field bedecked with banners and bright pavilions. Emerging from their palatial tents, the two kings walked toward each other—Richard escorted by two uncles of the king of France, Charles accompanied by their English counterparts. They passed between two lines of knights—400 French, 400 English—and embraced. At the moment of their meeting, the vast company of warriors fell to their knees, and many were moved to tears by the momentousness of the encounter.

POPES AND ANTIPOPES

The quiet dignity of this relief from the sarcophagus of Pope Urban VI, showing Urban receiving the papal key from Saint Peter, belies the bitter divisions that split the Roman Catholic church during his reign. The roots of the crisis stretched back to 1309, when Pope Clement V, a Frenchman, transferred the papacy from Rome to Avignon, a papal fief adjoining French territory. His successors followed his example and gave consistent support to France during the war against England, but the luxury and corruption of their court and the increasing power of its cardinals incurred widespread criticism: The Italian poet Petrarch, visiting Avignon in the 1340s, described it as "the Babylon of the West."

Responding to censure, Pope Gregory XI moved back to Rome in 1377, but his death the next year triggered an even greater crisis. The archbishop of Bari, an uncompromising advocate of papal power, was elected Urban VI; when he tried to curb the influence of the cardinals, however, they declared his election void and elevated one of their own number as Clement VII. Clement promptly returned to Avignon, while Urban continued in office in Rome.

During the ensuing decades of the Great Schism, which severely damaged the prestige of the papacy, the two popes proceeded to anathematize each other and excommunicate their rival's supporters. Political conflict and popular confusion were further aggravated in 1409, when the cardinals, seeking to break the deadlock, succeeded only in electing a third pontiff. A solution was reached in 1414 at the Council of Constance, which deposed or accepted the resignations of all three popes. The schism came to an end three years later with the election of Martin V.

In February, an old man flanked by flitches of bacon shares the warmth of a fire with his dog.

In March, a sower replenishes the bag of grain slung over his shoulder from sacks on the ground.

VIGNETTES OF DAILY LIFE

In several western European countries, including both England and France, the details of everyday fourteenth-century life were vividly captured in carvings on the wooden seats of church choirs. The images were fashioned beneath the ledges on the undersides of the seats known as misericords *(right)*; sitting was discouraged during prayers or offices and the seats were tipped up, but as a *misericordia*—"act of mercy"—they had narrow shelves that gave some support to the weary worshiper.

The choice of subject matter was usually left to the anonymous woodcarvers, who generally preferred secular to religious themes and often took the opportunity to display an irreverent wit in their art. The examples shown on these pages, from Worcester Cathedral in England, come from a sequence that illustrates seasonal activities associated with the twelve months of the year.

Reapers bind their sheaves with bands of wheat in August.

In October, a swineherd knocks acorns from a tree to fatten his hogs before the November slaughter.

A month later, to complete the pact, the wedding between the two royal houses was celebrated at Calais. The seven-year-old princess Isabelle, arrayed in emeralds and a scarlet velvet gown, was duly married to her English fiancé by the archbishop of Canterbury. It was agreed that the consummation of the match should be postponed until the bride achieved the riper age of twelve.

To the wedding guests, it may have seemed that Venus, the goddess of love, had finally brought an end to the grisly reign of Mars, the god of war. But the new century would bring proof that their optimism was unfounded. The moist-eyed knights at Calais might have done better to save their tears: Within two decades, their sons would be at one another's throats again.

A few years after the wedding, the throne of England was usurped by Henry IV, who forced Richard II to abdicate, and France was in chaos. Charles VI, whose mental health had progressively deteriorated, now labored under the illusion that he was made of glass and spent his days in nervous near-seclusion, terrified that he might shatter. In the ensuing power vacuum, a bitter rivalry erupted between the dukes of Burgundy and Orléans, two of the most powerful peers of France. After the assassination of Orléans by agents of the duke of Burgundy in 1407, the conflict escalated into civil war. Both parties attempted to deal secretly with the English, who chose to fan the flames by giving covert support to each side.

English troops were once again marching into France as the new king of England, Henry V, confidently presented his demands. He asked for a return of all those parts of Aquitaine lost to his predecessors in the course of the war, as well as the territories held by his own French ancestors—Normandy, Anjou, Touraine, Maine, and Ponthieu. In addition, he sought the hand of the mad king's daughter. If these desires were not fulfilled, he was prepared to invade.

Enjoying great popular support at home, Henry persuaded Parliament to grant him a massive subsidy for his campaign. He raised a sizable army and navy, shrugged off a newly discovered plot against his life, and set sail for France in 1415. His burning and pillaging of the war-weary regions of Normandy and Picardy were as brutal as anything perpetrated by his predecessors: War without fire, he often told his comrades-in-arms, was like a sausage without mustard. By the time he met the French army at Agincourt, his men were tired, cold, and plagued by illness; nevertheless, he was able to spur them to a victory against the odds.

Within five years, Henry V, supported by the duke of Burgundy, had occupied Paris. Yet the tide would eventually turn. The French, weary of English oppression, gradually recovered their confidence. Their forces in the north were inspired by the patriotic fervor of Joan of Arc, a peasant girl who donned armor and joined the fray. But they were not dependent solely on the charisma of the Maid of Orléans. Their military skills improved, and the genius of a civilian gunsmith, Maître Jean Bureau, provided them with firepower far superior to that of their enemies. Armed with his gunpowder and formidable artillery, they succeeded in conquering even Gascony.

No peace treaty would be signed until 1492. Even then, the English would not officially abandon their claims to their former lands; indeed, the English kings continued to call themselves kings of France on official documents until 1815. But by the end of the fifteenth century, the relationship between France and England had altered forever, and this old feudal quarrel had ceased to be an issue worthy of all-out war. At the price of uncountable quantities of blood, the Hundred Years' War had forged in both kingdoms a new sense of national identity.

THE RISE OF THE OTTOMANS

During the night of March 2, 1354, the western bank of the Dardanelles—the narrow strait between the Sea of Marmara and the Aegean that separates Europe from Asia— was devastated by an earthquake. The walls of the citadel of Gallipoli collapsed, and while most of the inhabitants fled in terror through driving rain and blizzards, the town was quickly occupied by an enemy army that had recently taken possession of a minor fortress in the region. Gallipoli was a stronghold of the Christian empire of Byzantium; the opportunists who seized it were Ottoman Turks, subjects of an Islamic state that had just recently risen to prominence on the Asiatic side of the strait. For the Ottoman sultan, the earthquake signified divine approval for his holy war against all Christian nations: "God having manifested His will in my favor by causing the ramparts to fall," he is alleged to have said, "my troops have taken possession of the city, penetrated with thanks to Allah."

Excepting only the Mongols in the thirteenth century, the Ottomans were the sole Asian people in this millennium to found an empire on the continent of Europe. Within fifty years of the seizure of Gallipoli, their first permanent foothold in Europe, they had occupied most of the Balkan lands; Constantinople, the capital of the Byzantine Empire, was completely surrounded, and the crushing defeat of an army of European Crusaders at Nicopolis on the Danube River had placed all of Christian Europe at their mercy.

Yet less than a century before Gallipoli, the Ottomans were an obscure tribal people no different from the other seminomadic warrior groups who inhabited the northwestern corner of Anatolia. Legend relates that this tribe was originally called the Kayi and was descended from the Oghuz Turks, a confederation of steppe-born nomads who had migrated westward from their central Asian homeland in the eighth century, embraced Islam, and during the eleventh century, under the Seljuk clan, established an empire of their own, covering Persia, Iraq, Syria, and Anatolia. This empire broke up during the twelfth century, and in 1243, the Seljuks in Anatolia were defeated by Mongol warriors at the Battle of Kose Dagh and reduced to vassal status.

At this time, so tradition has it, the Kayi tribe was led by Sulayman Shah, ruler of a small territory in northeast Persia. To avoid death or enslavement at the hands of the Mongol invaders, Sulayman fled westward with his people but was drowned while crossing the Euphrates into Syria. After his death, one of his sons, Ertoghrul, led some 400 followers farther west into Anatolia, where he came upon a battle between Turks and Mongols. Chivalrously entering the fray on the losing side, he tilted the scales in the Turks' favor and ensured their victory. By a stroke of providence, they proved to be the troops of the Seljuk sultan, who was so grateful for Ertoghrul's intervention that he awarded the chieftain a small fief around the village of Sogut, in the far northwest of Anatolia, and pastures at nearby Eskishehir (Old City).

The light of the setting sun silhouettes the domes and minarets of the fifteenth-century Yesil Cami mosque in Bursa, the city in what is now Turkey that was seized by the Ottomans in 1326 and became the capital of their expanding empire. After crushing the outposts of the Byzantine Empire in Asia Minor, the Ottoman warriors swept across the strait of the Dardanelles into Europe, overrunning most of the Balkan lands. The Ottomans left their stamp on their conquered territories not with castles or palaces, but with many-domed mosques such as this one, around which were grouped religious colleges, bathhouses, and soup kitchens to feed the poor.

There are many variations of this apocryphal tale, all calculated to establish for the Ottomans a legitimate connection with the illustrious Seljuk dynasty. More than likely, however, Ertoghrul and his followers were rootless nomads who, having fled to Anatolia to escape the Mongols, were then forcibly driven into the frontier regions around Sogut and Eskishehir by Seljuk leaders nervous of the impact such uncivilized aliens would have on their sophisticated state.

The region where Ertoghrul resettled was a rugged mountainous zone between the plateau of central Anatolia and the coastal plains. Seminomadic tribes similar to those led by Ertoghrul made up most of its population, and its culture was very different from the advanced civilization that had grown up in the Seljuk capital of Konya, two to three weeks' journey to the southeast. Its laws were those of the tribal past, not of the Muslim Koran. Its literature was epic and exclusively Turkish, in contrast to the refined Persian literature of the Seljuks. Its religion was a hybrid blend of orthodox Islam, heterodox mysticism, and ancient Turkish shamanism, and it even contained certain Christian elements. Its chieftains were warriors who had proved their mettle

This map shows the extent of Ottoman territory prior to the Turks' entry into Europe, which followed their capture of Gallipoli in 1354. Beginning as a small principality of nomadic Muslim warriors in northwest Anatolia, the Ottomans had conquered by the end of the century an empire whose borders stretched from the Danube in Europe to the east of Anatolia. After seizing Gallipoli on the west bank of the Dardanelles, they advanced to Adrianople, which was renamed Edirne, and proceeded to capture all the major cities of the Balkans. The Serbians were defeated at Kosovo in 1389, and the Hungarians and an army of Christian knights from western Europe were overwhelmed at Nicopolis on the Danube in 1396.

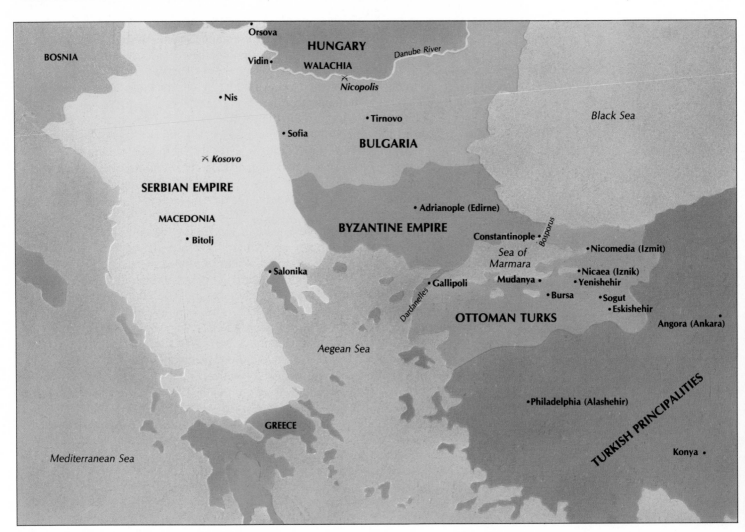

in raids against the coastal territory that belonged to the Byzantine Empire.

Dominating this frontier culture—as it was to dominate the culture of the Ottomans themselves—was the Islamic concept of *ghaza,* or "holy war." By God's command, the ghaza had to be fought against all Christian dominions—the *dar al-harb,* or "abode of war"—until they submitted. Islamic law permitted the seizure of property and the enslavement or killing of all captives taken during such warfare. To become a ghazi, a champion of holy war and leader of a band of dedicated followers, an aspiring warrior had to possess courage, strength of arm, determination, a good horse, a bow and arrows, a strong sword, a lance, and a faithful retainer. A ghazi who won an important victory over the Christians was proclaimed a bey, or prince, by the Seljuk sultan and received the symbols of authority: a robe, flag, horse, and drum.

Whether Ertoghrul himself achieved this distinction is not recorded. He died around 1280, bequeathing his small fief to his son Osman, called Uthman in Arabic. Since the ghazi groups were named after their leaders, the warriors who fought under his banner assumed the title Osmanlis, or Ottomans.

Osman was about thirty years old when he took his inheritance. The first accounts of his career were written long after his death, and by then he had become the stuff of legend. One of the earliest stories tells how he received a blessing from Sheik Edebali, who was probably the head of a popular dervish order. Practicing rites that often included the excitation of religious ecstasy through music, dancing, or drugs, dervish societies adhered to a mystical strain of Islam that had wide appeal among the poor, and Sheik Edebali was one of the most influential men in the region. Osman wanted to marry Edebali's daughter, but the sheik refused. Then one day the young warrior told the sheik about a dream in which he had seen a tree growing out of his loins with leaves that lengthened into sword blades and pointed in the direction of Constantinople. Edebali was well versed in the interpretation of dreams, and the message of this one seemed clear enough. Predicting that Osman's descendants would rule the world, Edebali gave his daughter's hand in marriage and personally girded Osman with a ghazi's sword—a weapon that would be worn by every Ottoman ruler for generations to come.

Edebali's faith in his son-in-law might have seemed misplaced to more cautious observers, for Osman's domain at the time could have been crossed on horseback in a single day. One of the smallest of about ten petty principalities in Anatolia, it appeared of slight significance compared with the Byzantine Empire to the west and that of the Mongols to the east. But there were two factors that Osman and his descendants could exploit to their unique advantage. The first was the strategic location of Osman's territory, right on the borders of the Byzantine Empire and within easy reach of the sea and the lands of Balkan Europe beyond it. The second was the Byzantine emperor's preoccupation with his enemies to the west, which caused him to neglect his eastern frontier.

At the beginning of the thirteenth century, the Comnenus dynasty of Byzantium had been overthrown by the armies of the Fourth Crusade, and large parts of the empire had been divided up among the conquerors. Constantinople was recaptured in 1261 by Michael VIII Palaeologus, the founder of the Palaeologus dynasty, but continued opposition from his western neighbors—Serbia, Bulgaria, northern Greece, and Venice—had compelled Michael to transfer many of his Anatolian frontier forces to Europe. There remained just three important Byzantine strongholds in Anatolia, all within a couple of days' march of Osman's base at Eskishehir. To the south lay Bursa, which was built on a fertile plain beneath the slopes of a mountain; in the center, at the head of a lake, stood Nicaea (present-day Iznik); to the north was the port of Nicomedia (today's Izmit), commanding the sea route to Constantinople and the overland route to the Black Sea.

Despite the proximity of these rich targets, Osman made no attempt to take them during the first twenty years of his reign. Conscious of his own relative weakness, he bided his time, directing his military activities against small border garrisons during the winter and retiring to the highland pastures during the summer. Meanwhile, his forces grew in number, reinforced not only by the recruitment of Turkish immigrants but also by the defection of Greek frontier warriors disgusted by Constantinople's negligent attitude. In 1299, when his army had grown substantially—by repute to some 4,000 troops—Osman made his first strategic move: By transferring his operational base to a township he renamed Yenishehir (New City), midway between Bursa and Nicaea, he severed communications between those two cities.

The first clash between Osman's warriors and a Byzantine army occurred in 1301. That year the emperor sent an army of about 2,000—mostly foreign mercenaries—to relieve ghazi pressure on Nicomedia. In a valley north of the city, they encountered an Ottoman raiding party. Possibly the Ottomans were ambushed or cut off from their base to the east, for instead of fighting defensively, deploying the characteristic Turkish tactics of harassing the enemy with their archers before engaging at close quarters, they mounted an impetuous charge that broke the Byzantine line.

When news of Osman's victory spread, ghazis from throughout Anatolia flocked to his banner. According to later Ottoman accounts, it was for this feat of arms that the Seljuk sultan in Konya proclaimed him a bey, ruler of an independent principality.

From his new base at Yenishehir, Osman directed the striking power of his ghazis in two directions—north toward the Black Sea and west toward the Sea of Marmara. Before the end of the first decade of the fourteenth century, his troops had appeared on the Bosporus, within sight of Constantinople, and also farther south along the coast of the Sea of Marmara, cutting off access to Bursa by land. In 1317, Osman laid siege to Bursa and in 1321 captured its main port of Mudanya. Starved of both supplies and military support from the Byzantine capital, Bursa finally surrendered in 1326. The city's commander, Evrenos, embraced the Muslim faith and joined the Ottoman army, subsequently becoming one of its greatest commanders.

Shortly after the occupation of Bursa, its conqueror died and was buried there, in a tomb facing Constantinople. His epitaph was embodied in a prayer that marked the accession of all future Ottoman rulers: "May he be as good as Osman," cried the assembled courtiers, as the new sultan was girded with his double-edged ghazi sword. Osman had led his people out of tribal anonymity and given them a distinctive and confident identity. He had assembled an army whose military strength matched its troops' religious fervor, and in the capture of Bursa, he had acquired for the Ottomans a secure base from which to consolidate and extend their conquests.

Osman's successor, chosen by the leading men of the realm, was the younger of his two sons, Orhan. About forty years old, Orhan had proved his military capacities during the protracted siege of Bursa. Orhan is reputed to have offered to share his rule with his elder brother, Ala al-Din, a scholarly and peaceful man. Ala al-Din declined, whereupon Orhan declared: "Since you will not rule, be my vizier, and bear the burdens of the organization of the state."

As Orhan's chief minister, Ala al-Din devoted the rest of his life to the administration of the Ottoman lands, which by now included almost all the northwestern corner of Anatolia. Bursa was ideally situated to become both the political and the commercial capital. During the thirteenth century, Anatolia had become a crossing point and center of exchange for both east-west and north-south trade routes; as the Ottoman armies advanced during the course of the century and more caravan routes came under their control, Bursa became an increasingly important commercial center. Fine woolen cloths arrived from Europe, and silks from Persia and China; furs and slaves from the Mongol khanate of the Golden Horde to the north were exchanged for spices, sugar, and fabrics from the Arab lands to the south. The profits from such trade fueled both the civic and the military development of the Ottoman enterprise.

This manuscript illustration of the Islamic angel Shamhurshat was included in an astrological treatise prepared in 1272 for a sultan of the Seljuk dynasty, the most powerful rulers in Anatolia before the emergence of the Ottomans. Although the Seljuks, like the Ottomans, were Muslims, the holy man's sword and details of the horse's harness resemble those of a Christian knight. The image shows how thoroughly Eastern and Western influences were mingled in Anatolia at the time of the foundation of the Ottoman state: On the borders of the Byzantine Empire, Christian and Islamic traditions were not always distinct, and the affinities between this angel and the Christian Saint George—one of several warrior saints of Christendom popular in the Middle East—were not accidental.

Byzantine traditions helped to shape many aspects of the newly forged Ottoman culture. Greeks were employed in administrative positions, and court etiquette was influenced by the captured Byzantine women who formed a substantial proportion of the harem kept by the Ottoman sultan in the royal palace; in addition, the Ottomans took over many Greek practices in cooking, crafts, and shipbuilding. The influence of the Seljuks was also apparent, both in the administration—for which Ala al-Din recruited jurists from the Seljuk lands—and in the architecture of the mosques, almshouses, and caravansaries built by the Ottomans in the towns that they had conquered. In other matters, however, Orhan and his brother made clear their intention to create a distinctive Ottoman society. Rejecting the title of bey, which implied that he was merely a Seljuk vassal, Orhan took the titles Sultan, son of the Sultan of the Ghazis, Ghazi son of Ghazi, Marquis of the Horizons, Hero of the World. Coins were minted bearing the name of Orhan as well as the motto: "May God prolong his rule." The Turkish language was used for official matters and, from the middle of the century, for Ottoman literature. The traditional Turkish *tughra,* originally a nomad brand mark for horses, evolved into beautiful and complex works of calligraphy that served as royal signatures on state documents.

Sunni Islam was adopted as the state religion, but Orhan and his vizier owed much to the activities of the various dervish orders of Anatolia. In the frontier regions, they

51

actively supported warfare against the infidel and also founded hospices for travelers that supported resident communities somewhat in the manner of Christian monasteries. In newly conquered territory, the dervish orders were permitted to select a plot of land and build a hospice endowed by the ruler. Because those who lived in the hospice communities received tax exemptions, immigrants from more-settled areas of Anatolia flocked to join them, helping swell the population on the frontier. The majority of the Turkish villages that were established in the fourteenth century originated as dervish hospices.

In the towns, societies of artisans and merchants founded similar rest houses for travelers besides looking after the social welfare of their own members. These sects, which had close links with dervish orders, were led by people called *ahis*. Ibn-Battuta, the celebrated Moorish traveler, visited Anatolia in 1333 and expressed his admiration for their work: "Nowhere in the world are there to be found any to compare with them in solicitude for strangers and in ardor to serve to satisfy wants."

Ibn-Battuta was invited by one such ahi—a cobbler in shabby clothes—to visit his hospice, which had been built by about 200 men of different trades who paid for its upkeep by contributing from their wages. Among his hosts, he noted young men wearing white woolen caps with a flap hanging down the back—the uniform headgear of the ahi societies, later to be adopted by the elite troops of the Ottoman army. When he had taken his place among them, he was regaled with fruit and sweets, after which he was entertained by singing and dancing. "Everything about them filled us with admiration," ibn-Battuta wrote, "and we were greatly astonished at their generosity and innate nobility."

When he reached Bursa, described by ibn-Battuta as a "fine and populous city with fine bazaars and wide streets," the traveler was received by Orhan himself—"the greatest of the Turkmen kings, and the richest in wealth, lands, and military forces. Of fortresses he possesses nearly 100, and for most of his time he is continually engaged in making the rounds of them. It is said that he has never stayed for a whole month in any town. He also fights with the infidels continually and keeps them under siege." Like his father, Orhan remained true to the ghazi ethic, ruling from the saddle rather than the palace.

Orhan's army was a far more professional force than that commanded by his father. Osman's army had consisted exclusively of irregular cavalry, called *akinjis* (raiders) or *delis* (fanatics), who were recruited for a campaign by heralds who rode around the villages issuing a call to arms. These akinjis were retained by Orhan as an advance guard of shock troops who were sent deep into enemy territory to pulverize the border defenses and terrorize the population. In a pitched battle, however, Orhan placed an irregular and expendable infantry force in the forefront of the Ottoman army to absorb the enemy's first attacks. If that gave way, the enemy found himself faced by a force of regular salaried troops and archers organized in units of 10, 100, and 1,000. The elite troops were the regular cavalry, called *sipahis*, drawn from the sultan's close comrades in arms and rewarded for their services by the grant of nonhereditary fiefs in conquered territory.

Discipline in the Ottoman army was fierce and training strict. When European opponents first encountered the Ottoman troops, they were amazed by the speed and silence with which they marched. "They can start suddenly," wrote one French eyewitness, "and 100 Christian soldiers would make more noise than 10,000 Osmanlis. When the drum sounded, they put themselves immediately in march, never breaking step, never stopping till the word is given. Lightly armed, in one night they travel as far as their Christian adversaries in three days." Special attention was paid to developing the native Turkish skills of mounted archery and javelin throwing; the unwieldy firearms that were beginning to be introduced in Europe did not appear in the Ottoman army until the end of the century and remained uncommon until the sixteenth century.

With such a formidable military machine, Orhan had little difficulty swallowing up Nicaea in 1331 and Nicomedia in 1337, leaving the Byzantines only a tenuous foothold on the peninsula that stood opposite Constantinople. He also extended his frontiers to the southwest, annexing the principality of Karasi, which gave him command of the south coast of the Sea of Marmara and the Dardanelles. Across this narrow strait stood Gallipoli, an important Byzantine stronghold as well as a gateway to Europe. By the middle of the century, Orhan was ready to turn his ghazis on the Christians in their own realms.

Like most of Europe at this period, the southeastern corner was a bitterly divided region, fragmented by dynastic quarrels and trade wars, depopulated by famine and plague, torn apart by rivalry between the Greek Orthodox patriarch in Constantinople and the Catholic pope in Rome. To the west of Byzantine territory—which consisted of an area roughly equivalent to modern European Turkey—Stephen Dushan had created the fragile empire of Serbia, today part of northern Greece and southern Yugoslavia. To the north of Serbia was Bosnia, which in 1353 had won its independence from the kingdom of Hungary, the largest and most powerful state in the region and the only one whose rulers professed allegiance to the Roman Catholic faith. North of Byzantium was Bulgaria, which had been conquered by Serbia in 1330; beyond the Danube was Walachia, now part of Rumania, which in the same year had broken away from Hungary.

Orhan did not have to force his way into Europe; he was invited there. On his deathbed in 1341, the Byzantine emperor Andronicus III had named his chancellor, Cantacuzene, guardian of his young son, John Palaeologus, and coregent with his wife, Empress Anna. Dissatisfied with this arrangement, Cantacuzene proclaimed himself sole emperor in 1343, then appealed to Orhan for military aid against his opponents. In return, he offered to give Orhan his daughter Theodora in marriage. Flattered perhaps by the prospect of a family connection with the Byzantine royal house, Orhan accepted, and with the aid of 6,000 Ottoman troops, Cantacuzene first gained control of the coastal towns of the Black Sea and then, in 1347, of Constantinople itself. Forced to come to terms, Anna agreed that Cantacuzene and Palaeologus should reign as coemperors, the usurper being recognized as senior emperor for ten years, after which they would rule as equals.

The unlikely alliance between Cantacuzene and Orhan established a dangerous precedent. In 1349, Cantacuzene and his coemperor again called on Ottoman assistance, this time to relieve the Greek port of Salonika, which was being besieged by Stephen Dushan of Serbia. An army of 20,000 Ottoman troops crossed into Byzantine territory, accomplished their task, and then returned home. Two years later, Cantacuzene made a third appeal, this time for assistance in the civil war that had broken out after John Palaeologus, now of age, had claimed his birthright. Cantacuzene paid for this assistance with spoils from the churches of Constantinople, and he promised to reward his Ottoman son-in-law with a fortress on the European side of the Dardanelles.

Written in July 1348, this document recording the grant of an estate to an army commander is signed at the top by Orhan, who ruled the Ottomans from 1326 to 1360. The stylized signatures of Ottoman rulers were known as *tughras;* evolved from marks of ownership used to brand their horses, these signatures developed into ornate works of calligraphy in later centuries. The document is written in Persian, used during the early years of Ottoman rule for official government purposes; Arabic was the language of religion, and Turkish was the tongue of everyday life.

Early in 1352, Orhan sent his eldest son, Sulayman, to take possession of the promised fortress, a minor stronghold called Tzympe in the region of Gallipoli. Sulayman reinforced his position by transporting more Ottoman troops across the strait of the Dardanelles, and in 1354, after the earthquake that struck the western bank had destroyed the defenses of Gallipoli itself, he was able to occupy this major fortress unopposed. Cantacuzene's demand for the return of Gallipoli was met by a flat refusal, and the first colony of Ottoman settlers was brought over to Europe.

Outraged public opinion compelled Cantacuzene to declare war on his former ally, but his appeal to the kings of Serbia and Bulgaria for help was rejected with scorn. "Three years ago," the king of Bulgaria replied, "I remonstrated with you for your unholy alliance with the Turks. Now that the storm has broken, let the Byzantines weather it. If the Turks come against us, we shall know how to defend ourselves." Utterly discredited, Cantacuzene had no choice but to abdicate in favor of John Palaeologus. He retired to a monastery, allowing John to become the undisputed ruler of Byzantium by 1357.

That year, Sulayman was killed in a fall from a horse while out hawking, but his younger brother, Murad, advanced north from Gallipoli and laid siege to Adrianople. Succeeding his father, Orhan, as the Ottoman ruler in 1360, Murad was at first distracted from consolidating the Ottoman foothold in Europe by a rebellion in Angora (Ankara, modern Turkey's capital). The merchant guilds of this town had determined to win their independence from Ottoman rule in alliance with the Karaman principality around Konya. In two swift campaigns, Murad crushed the rebels, then crossed back into Europe. When Adrianople finally surrendered in 1361, Murad renamed this city Edirne and made it the main Ottoman base in Europe. He now commanded the strongest fort between Constantinople and the Danube, and the route to the Balkans lay open before him.

By now, the Ottoman advance was sending tremors throughout Europe. However, Pope Urban V's appeal for a Crusade of Catholic Christians to rescue Byzantium met with little enthusiasm. The Catholic nations of Europe had their own more immediate problems, and besides, most of them loathed the Greek church. Their general attitude was summed up by the Italian poet Petrarch who, writing to Urban in 1364, actually recommended that the Ottomans be used to wipe out the Eastern heresy. "The Osmanlis are merely enemies," he wrote, "but the schismatic Greeks are worse than enemies. The Osmanlis hate us less, for they fear us less. The Greeks, however, both fear and hate us with all their soul."

The only Catholic ruler to respond to the pope's call was Amadeus VI, duke of Savoy, who led a fleet to Gallipoli and recaptured it in 1366. His price for returning it to Byzantium was the Greek emperor's submission to the Roman Catholic church. When John Palaeologus resisted, explaining that his people would depose him, Amadeus threatened to hand Gallipoli back to the Ottomans and unleash his own soldiers on the Byzantines. Finally, John agreed and Amadeus returned to Italy, carrying some of the emperor's private jewels and other securities to the pope in person as pledges of his submission.

Byzantium itself literally could not afford to stand alone against the Ottoman menace. Its currency had been devalued, its trade revenues were mostly controlled by the Genoese, and the crown jewels had been pawned to the Venetians. To pay for a larger army, John attempted to take over land owned by the Orthodox church, but the patriarch refused to cooperate. In 1369, John was at last persuaded to honor his

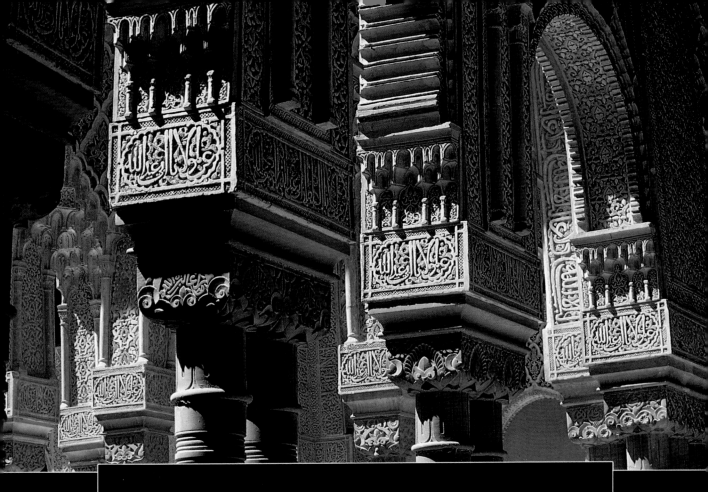

ISLAM IN SPAIN

At the time of the Ottoman irruption into Europe, the only other Muslim power on the continent had been reduced, after six centuries of reconquest, to a single outpost in the rugged mountains of southern Andalusia in Spain. Under the protective suzerainty of Christian Castile, however, the Nasrid dynasty of Granada transformed the citadel that dominated their capital into a defiant assertion of Islamic civilization.

The Alhambra—literally "red"—palace within previously constructed pink stone walls that gave it its name. The maze of royal apartments and audience halls was richly ornamented with painted wood, mosaic tile, and stucco—a plaster containing gypsum or lime and fine sand—which lent itself to such intricate work as that on the arches surrounding the courtyard (above). Since figurative portrayal was not approved by many Muslims, the interwoven decorative motifs were derived from geom-

Surmounting a densely wooded hill, the stark outer defenses of the Alhambra present an impregnable obstacle to any would-be attacker. The walls were extensively restored in the thirteenth century by the founder of the Nasrid dynasty, and round artillery bastions were added to the Citadel *(above, right)* during the fifteenth century. But the chief architectural glories of the Nasrid builders were the domestic and ceremonial buildings, including the Hall of the Ambassadors *(above, center)*, whose stark facade belies the sumptuous elegance of its interior.

The sloping tiled roofs, cool arcades, and delicate surface decoration of the Court of the Lions, which takes its name from the twelve bronze lions surrounding the central fountain, were probably designed purely for sensuous pleasure rather than for any official function. The fountain's water sprayed out from the lions' mouths and flowed along channels into the neighboring halls.

Arches and columns frame the inner palace gardens, which contained cypresses and orange trees. The play of light and shade and reflections from polished floors or pools of water invited the eye to lose itself in the intricacy of the stucco decoration, and the mind to contemplate the infinite wonder of God's creation. Below the stucco stretched echoing patterns of colorful tiles.

promise to go to Rome, and on October 21, the emperor of the Greeks declared his allegiance to the Catholic church in a brilliant ceremony that ended with his genuflecting before the pope and kissing the pontiff's feet.

This conversion was an individual act that applied only to the emperor himself, and all that he received in return were pious generalizations from the pope about the benefits that would follow, and the return of his jewels from Amadeus. After five months, the hapless John set off for home, only to be arrested for debt and detained by the Venetians. To add to his wretchedness, his elder son refused to pay the ransom, and it was several months before his younger son managed to raise the money to bail him out. John finally reached his capital two years after his departure; he had nothing to show for his efforts, however, and the Byzantine church remained steadfastly Orthodox.

Any hopes that John may have cherished of help from the Catholic powers in the Balkans were crushed by the Ottoman defeat of an army of Serbians and Hungarians in 1371. Motivated by fear of what would happen to their Catholic realms if Murad succeeded in crossing the Balkans, these nations sent an allied expedition to attack Edirne; the army was surprised by an Ottoman night attack just after they had crossed the Maritza River, however, and, in the words of a Turkish historian, the Christians "were driven as flames are driven before the wind till, plunging into the Maritza, they perished in its waters." Bereft of allies, John Palaeologus had no choice but to conclude an agreement with Murad whereby he agreed to pay tribute and supply military aid to the Ottomans.

Over the next two decades, Murad extended Ottoman rule over the Balkans in a series of strategically planned campaigns. Local Christian princes were turned into vassals, forced to send their sons to the Ottoman court as hostages, to pay tribute, and to serve in Ottoman expeditions against their fellow Christians. The Ottoman advance was facilitated not only by rivalries among these princes—many of whom were happy to fight with the Ottomans against their neighbors—but also by a lack of resistance from the peasantry who, living on feudal holdings and subject to repressive taxes and dues, had little motive to defend their overlords. These lands were now brought under direct Ottoman control and were assigned to the sipahis only by the sultan's personal decree and in accordance with tax regulations executed by a local Ottoman official acting independently of the fief holder. For many peasants, the new regime was an improvement. For example, the feudal code of the Serbian monarch Stephen Dushan had required the peasant to work for his lord two days a week, whereas Ottoman laws stipulated that subjects of the empire must work only three days a year on the sipahis' land.

Murad also demonstrated wise statecraft by adopting a tolerant attitude toward the Christian religion, even going so far as to officially recognize the Orthodox church—a move designed to widen the schism between Rome and Constantinople and thus reduce the chances of a Western Crusade being mounted. Although he was the leader of a holy war dedicated to spreading Islam throughout the world, he was too pragmatic to enforce wholesale conversion; following the established practice of Muslim conquerors since the time of Muhammad, Murad guaranteed protection to his Christian subjects provided they did not subvert Muslim rule and paid a special poll tax in lieu of performing military service. Those who did fight for the Ottomans under the command of Christian vassal princes received tax exemptions and small land grants.

Murad's willingness to accept Christian soldiers suggests that he could not find

A mosaic from the church of Saint Savior in Constantinople shows its chief benefactor, Theodore Metochites, presenting a model of the church to Christ. Although the dwindling treasury of the Byzantine Empire curbed the production of gold and silver ornaments in the fourteenth century, many of its finest mosaics and frescoes were produced at that time. Metochites served for many years as the empire's chief executive official, but he later fell from grace and became a monk in the monastery attached to the church he had restored.

sufficient recruits in his thinly populated Islamic lands, but he doubted the loyalty of infidels who fought for money alone and who remained under the control of non-Muslim commanders. His solution was to raise a new military force composed of formerly Christian slaves who were directly under his control. In Islamic law, the enslavement of Muslims was forbidden, but it was permissible to convert members of other religions who had already been enslaved. Murad had other reasons for preferring such converts to a personal guard of Turks who, "if they were to become slaves of the sultan," an Ottoman source explained, "would abuse this privilege. Their relatives in the province would oppress the taxpaying subjects and not pay taxes. They would oppose the governors and become rebels. But if Christian children accept Islam, they become zealous in their faith and enemies of their relatives."

According to some legends, it was Orhan who had established the first slave corps, calling its members "slaves of the porte"—because in principle they were always at the door of the sultan's tent, ready to do his bidding. In fact, it is more likely that the first recruits were Christian boys captured after the conquest of Adrianople. Whatever its origins, the system was to prove extremely effective. Transported to Bursa, likely looking candidates were educated in Turkish and the tenets of Islam at the same time as they were taught the crafts of war. When their religious and military education had been completed, the recruits were organized as an infantry corps, the *Yeni Ceri*, or

New Force, familiar to Europeans in future generations as the janissaries.

Murad was able to enlarge the force by claiming his share of the army's booty in the form of raw janissary recruits. He also instituted the practice of *devshirme,* the "gathering of the youths," a periodical conscription of Christian boys in the Balkans, with the best being entered into the army or palace service. Local taxpaying subjects were compelled to pay for the cost of transporting their conscripted sons and brothers to the training barracks.

As the janissary force grew, it was split into divisions, each distinguished by a symbol such as an anchor, a key, or a fish. Some men even had the divisional sign tattooed on their bodies. In their mess halls, the divisions congregated around huge copper cauldrons, and gradually these pots acquired an arcane significance of their own: If one of them was ever lost in battle, all the officers of the division were dismissed and never again accepted into the same company. The culinary symbolism also carried through into the titles of the officers, a colonel being known as a "chief soup maker," a quartermaster a "chief cook," and so on down to "water carriers" and "kitchen scullions." These names were probably inspired by the duties handed out to janissary recruits during the early history of the force. Promotion through the ranks was by length of service, and all members received a monthly salary and a pension upon retirement.

Another distinctive characteristic of the janissaries was their adherence to the dervish order of the Bektashis, founded in the late thirteenth century by a mystic named Hajji Bektash. Incorporating many heterodox elements that made it attractive to Christian and Muslim alike, the cult was popular throughout the Ottoman heartland. In its rites, the drinking of alcohol was permitted and women could participate, unveiled, on equal terms. Initiates joined a lodge and held convivial gatherings whose laxity shocked the Sunni. The janissaries made Bektash their patron saint and recruited Bektashis as chaplains, and one regiment had a Bektashi sheik—or spiritual leader—as its colonel. The Christian elements of the Bektashis' ceremonial may have been introduced by the janissaries themselves, as a dim echo of their religious heritage. They identified their patron saint with Greek Orthodox saints, and some janissaries went into battle carrying biblical quotations as lucky charms.

Removed far from home, forbidden to marry, prevented from engaging in any trade, the janissaries gave their loyalty exclusively to each other and to their royal master. With their aid, Murad had little difficulty in capturing the major cities of the Balkans: Bitolj in Macedonia in 1380, Sofia in the central Balkans in 1385, Nis in Serbia in 1386, Salonika in 1387. Wherever the Ottoman army appeared, it seemed, victory was theirs for the taking.

However, the concentration of Ottoman forces in Europe left their Asian frontiers vulnerable, and a rising by the Karaman principality in Anatolia led indirectly to Murad's first significant defeat. The Karamans had established themselves in Konya on the central Anatolian plateau and regarded themselves as the heirs of the Seljuks; and in 1386, while Murad was campaigning in Europe, they seized their chance to occupy Ottoman territory. Murad returned posthaste with a force composed mainly of Greeks, Serbians, and Bulgarians mustered by his Christian vassals. After fighting an indecisive battle outside Konya, the Christian troops returned to their homelands, apparently disgusted because Murad had forbidden them to loot Turkish property. The return of these disgruntled soldiers encouraged the Serbian prince Lazar to stimulate resistance against the Ottomans. With the support of the prince of Bosnia and the king of Bulgaria, he formed a pan-Serbian alliance that crushed an Ottoman army at Plochnik in Bosnia in 1388. This victory made Lazar the rallying figure for Christian resistance throughout the Balkans.

Murad himself, now about seventy years old, was in Anatolia at the time of the Ottoman defeat, and he remained there for several months, waiting for his enemies to fall out among themselves. In the spring of 1389, he determined that the time was ripe for his revenge. First he conducted a lightning campaign against Bulgaria, establishing his rule right up to the Danube. Then he marched on Serbia with the troops of his Bulgarian vassal, Serbian rivals of Lazar, and the contingents of several Turkish princes. On June 15, 1389, the Ottoman army met Lazar's force on the plain of Kosovo—literally, "The Field of Blackbirds"—near the meeting point of the Serbian, Bosnian, and Albanian borders.

Murad was so confident of victory that he ordered his troops not to destroy any of the surrounding castles or villages after they had won the battle. The Serbians, on the other hand, showed signs of the disunity that Murad had hoped for: In a speech to his troops, Lazar publicly accused his son-in-law, Milosh Obravitch, of treason. And indeed, such disunity was to cost them the battle. Murad's forces attacked first, but the Serbians broke through the Ottomans' left flank of Asiatic troops and were checked only by the ferocity of Murad's son Bajazet, who led the right wing of European troops to the rescue. Then, at the critical moment, one of Lazar's allies deserted the field with some 12,000 men, so weakening the Serbians that they broke ranks and fled. Most of the troops were captured and killed, including Lazar; with him died hopes of an independent Serbian nation.

But Murad was dead, too—assassinated on the field of battle. Among the many legends surrounding this deed, the likeliest version claims that it was committed by Milosh Obravitch. Stung by his father-in-law's accusation of treachery, he pretended to desert to the Ottomans, gained an audience with the sultan, and then stabbed him with a concealed dagger.

News of Murad's death was greeted with joy by rulers in Christendom. In Florence, a *Te Deum* was sung, and in Paris, King Charles VI gave thanks to God in the church of Notre Dame. The response was a measure of the fear and awe that the sultan inspired in the West. Although his achievements were not so fully chronicled as those of his successors, he was perhaps the greatest ruler that the Ottoman dynasty produced. Just as Orhan had built on his father's deeds, welding a state out of the people unified by Osman, so Murad expanded his inheritance and laid the solid foundations for a multiracial, multireligious, and multilingual empire.

Murad had been renowned for his clemency toward his vanquished enemies. Almost the first act of his successor, Bajazet, was to order the murder of his younger brother, Yakub, a hero of Kosovo. Since Turkish tradition did not allow the blood of a noble to be spilled, Yakub was strangled with a bowstring. The new ruler attempted to justify the crime by citing a verse in the Koran: "So often as they return to sedition, they shall be subverted therein; and if they depart not from you, and offer you peace and restrain their hands from warring against you, take them and kill them wheresoever you find them." In the next century, fratricide by a succeeding Ottoman ruler was to become legal, and only in the seventeenth century did the siblings of a new sultan suffer the lesser fate of being locked up in isolation in the harem. Though inhuman, this custom helped ensure the unbroken survival of the dynasty and ex-

AN EMPIRE TORN ASUNDER

Toward the middle of the fourteenth century, when the Ottomans had already occupied its territories in Anatolia, the Byzantine Empire was riven by civil war. Hostilities commenced in 1341 on the death of Andronicus III, whose son and heir, John Palaeologus, was too young to rule in his own name. John VI Cantacuzene *(above, left)*, the late emperor's chancellor, proclaimed himself sole regent; he was opposed by the widow of Andronicus, Empress Anna, and by High Admiral Alexis Apokaukus *(above, right)*, who represented the interests of the common people against the aristocratic party of Cantacuzene.

Stephen Dushan of Serbia supported first one side and then the other, while Cantacuzene rashly invoked the aid of the Ottomans. After Apokaukus was killed in a riot in 1345, the war swung in favor of Cantacuzene, but by the time he entered Constantinople in triumph in 1347, the military strength of the empire was exhausted. The real victors were the Serbians and the Ottomans, between whom the future of Byzantium would be decided.

plains why there were only thirty-six Ottoman rulers during their 600-year history.

Bajazet was very different in temperament from his father. He inherited Murad's instinct for war and even eclipsed his ability to stage swift campaigns; because of the speed with which he could move an army between Europe and Asia, he was called *Yildirim* (the Thunderbolt). But he lacked his father's assurance, political guile, and tolerance, displaying instead an impetuous and cruel nature that made him many enemies. Merciless in the prosecution of war, he relaxed between campaigns by indulging in the sensuous pleasures of a court that resembled Byzantium in its degenerate heyday and that estranged him from the true ghazis.

Bajazet also differed from his father in his policy toward the other Turkish rulers in Anatolia, treating them as infidels and justifying attacks against them on the grounds that they had actively sabotaged the Ottomans' holy war on Christendom. Using the Karamans' overt hostility as a pretext, Bajazet returned from Europe intent on annexing each and every Turkish principality. He rapidly defeated the armies of most of these principalities and seized Konya from the Karamans, but at this point, his followers evinced so much displeasure at waging war on people of their own faith that Bajazet was obliged to accept Karaman peace proposals. To give an air of legitimacy to his conquests, he persuaded the Abbasid caliph in Cairo—Islam's spiritual leader—to confer on him the title of sultan of Rum, last held by the Seljuks, who had been the first Islamic rulers of the "Roman" lands wrested from Byzantium.

Before Bajazet could make any attempt to assimilate his Asian conquests, disturbing news from Constantinople made him hurry back to Europe. In February 1391, the ill-starred John Palaeologus had died. One of his last acts as an Ottoman vassal had been to assist at the siege of Philadelphia in Anatolia; as a fifteenth-century Byzantine historian acidly reported, the emperor of the Greeks distinguished himself by being the first over the walls when this last surviving Hellenic city in Asia was taken by the infidel. In 1390, he had made a belated gesture of defiance by ordering the strengthening of Constantinople's walls, but on receiving Bajazet's threat to blind his son Manuel, who was held hostage in Bursa, he had the fortifications demolished.

Immediately upon learning of his father's death, Manuel managed to slip secretly out of Bursa and hurry back to Constantinople, where he was crowned emperor. Furious that he had been denied a chance to appoint a Byzantine ruler of his own choice, Bajazet issued an ultimatum: "If you do not accept my orders and do as I command, then shut the gates of your city and govern what lies behind them; for everything beyond the gates belongs to me." The sultan's demands included the provision of a special quarter in Constantinople for Turkish merchants; a resident *qadi,* or judge, to arbitrate in their affairs with Christian residents; and a vast tribute that was beyond the resources of the Byzantine treasury. When these demands were not met, Bajazet put the city under siege. Seven months later, seeing no other way to save his inheritance, Manuel agreed to Bajazet's demands and ceded one-quarter of his city to Muslim settlers. From the minarets of two mosques, the Muslim call to prayer now rang out across Christian Constantinople.

Once Byzantium was subdued, Bajazet resumed his campaign in Anatolia, only to be distracted by a new threat from Europe. His Bulgarian vassal Sisman, supported by King Sigismund of Hungary, was attempting to throw off the Ottoman yoke, and in 1392, he captured the city of Nicopolis, the chief Ottoman stronghold on the Danube. Bajazet did not allow the rebellion to spread. A Turkish army regained Nicopolis later that year, then went on to take Tirnovo, the Bulgarian capital. Sisman was captured and later executed, for Bajazet had decided to break with his father's policy of ruling through vassals. From now on, Bulgaria would be an integral province of the empire, its people Ottoman subjects.

The capricious nature of Bajazet's ruthlessness was demonstrated in the winter of 1393-1394 when, to show what would befall his remaining Christian vassals if they revolted, he summoned to his court Manuel, together with other members of the Byzantine imperial family and Stephen Lazarevich of Serbia. Most imagined that they were going to be murdered. The emperor Manuel had no doubt. As he wrote later, "The tyrant thought the moment favorable to accomplish the massacre, which he had so long contemplated, so that, in his own words, having cleared the ground of thorns (meaning us), his own people would be able to dance on Christian soil without scratching their feet." Bajazet did in fact blind and cut off the hands of a few Byzantine officers, but then his mood changed and he tried to placate Manuel with gifts, "as one tries to calm a child's cries with sweets after one has beaten it."

Shaken but unharmed, Manuel returned to his capital convinced that nothing could be achieved by trying to negotiate with a man as willful and unpredictable as Bajazet. The next time the sultan demanded his presence at court, he ignored the summons, provoking Bajazet into sending an army to sack the outskirts of Constantinople and to impose a blockade that was to last from 1394 to 1402. Rejecting an offer of asylum in Venice, Manuel chose to sit out the siege, relying on the strength of the city walls and sure that a Western Crusade would soon be mounted.

For once, this was not mere wishful thinking—although the European rulers were concerned not so much with the plight of Byzantium as with the danger the Ottomans posed to Hungary, the last independent kingdom standing between Bajazet and the European heartlands. Direct rule of Bulgaria had brought Bajazet's forces to the Hungarian border, and in typically bombastic fashion, he had declared his intention to conquer the country and then proceed to Rome where, he promised, he would feed his horse with oats on the altar of Saint Peter's. King Sigismund's response was to canvass the Western Christian powers for a Crusade to "go against the Turks to their loss and destruction."

The pope in Rome replied to the Catholic king's plea with sympathy but no action, so Sigismund next sent an emissary to Paris. The French king, Charles VI, happened to be suffering from a temporary bout of madness, but his uncle, the duke of Burgundy, responded enthusiastically by raising a huge sum to finance a Crusade; he also rallied a great army of French, English, Scottish, German, and Italian knights, as well as adventurers from all over Europe and an auxiliary naval fleet manned by the Venetians, the Genoese, and the Christian military order of the Knights Hospitalers. This force—the most international gathering ever to take the cross against the infidel—joined with King Sigismund's own army at the Hungarian capital of Buda in July 1396. Roughly half of the Crusaders were under the command of King Sigismund, while the French contingent acknowledged the leadership of John, count of Nevers, the twenty-four-year-old son of the duke of Burgundy.

Sigismund, who had been expecting an Ottoman invasion since May, favored a defensive strategy designed to draw Bajazet into Hungary and destroy him. The Western nobility disdained such a passive and unchivalrous attitude, and by August, when there was still no sign of the promised Ottoman advance, they overrode Sigismund's protests and persuaded him to join them on a great offensive that would take them through the Balkans, Anatolia, and Syria and even on to Jerusalem itself.

The army accordingly marched down the Danube to Orsova, where it took eight days to ferry the troops across the narrow defile called the Iron Gates and into Serbia. Advancing into Ottoman-occupied Bulgaria, they captured Nis with great slaughter, continued east to the fortress of Vidin, where they massacred the Turkish garrison, and finally proceeded down the Danube River to Rahova, which contained many Bulgarian Christians. When the city surrendered, the Crusaders put the entire population to the sword, with the exception of about 1,000 wealthier inhabitants who were held for ransom.

At Nicopolis, the Christian forces received their first check. The Turkish stronghold was built beside the Danube on a hill crowned with a double line of imposing walls. Neither the Western Crusaders nor Sigismund, who had prepared only for a defensive campaign, was provided with siege equipment. When the first attempts to storm the walls failed, the army sat down to starve the city into surrender. The blockade was made more effective by the arrival of the Hospitalers fleet, which had sailed up the Danube from the Black Sea.

By now it was September, and still there was no news of Bajazet. The Crusaders grew restive and discipline broke down. The Western knights began to treat the operation as an exotic holiday, amusing themselves with gambling, drinking, and the local women. The few soldiers who suggested that such behavior was not the best preparation for battle against a foe as formidable as the Ottomans had their ears cut off for defeatism. Quarrels broke out between the various contingents, and some of Sigismund's vassals and allies talked openly of deserting.

Meanwhile, Bajazet, having heard of the Crusaders' arrival in Hungary, had broken off his siege of Constantinople and was marching with his usual swiftness toward the Danube. The first clash between the opposing forces occurred when the French lord of Coucy, impatient for reliable news of the enemy, led a reconnaissance party south of Nicopolis and encountered an advance contingent of the Ottoman army; luring them into a narrow defile, he ambushed the Turks and utterly routed them. But the effect of Coucy's surprise victory on his fellow knights was unfortunate: Roused from their drinking and carousing, they now became impetuous and overeager to do battle.

On September 25, 1396, Bajazet's army appeared in the hills some three miles from the Crusader camp. Well aware of the Ottomans' superb discipline and mobility, Sigismund advised caution and proposed that his Walachian foot soldiers be sent forward to encounter the vanguard of rough conscripts that were customarily placed to the fore of the Ottoman army—these were expendable troops and not worthy opponents, Sigismund argued, for the Crusader cavalry. The French knights

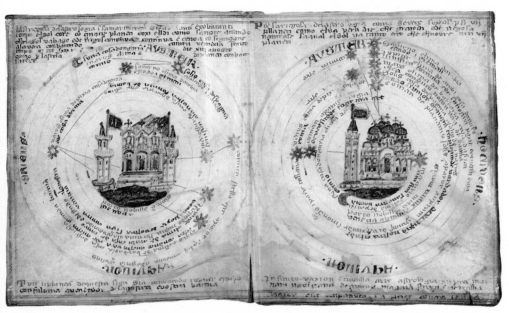

The buildings depicted in these vignettes from a late-fourteenth-century Venetian nautical chart are, on the left, the lighthouse and cathedral of Genoa, and on the right, the campanile—bell tower—and church of Saint Mark in Venice. According to the text, the configurations of stars and moon had a major influence on the outcome of a bitter struggle between these two merchant republics for control of the maritime trade routes through the straits of the Bosporus and the Dardanelles. The Genoese maintained a series of bases around Anatolia and the Black Sea, while Venice held possessions in Greece and the Aegean; both republics also became involved in the war between the Ottomans and the Byzantine Empire, who each sought to use the Italian fleets to their own advantage. In January 1380, after a battle lasting five months; the Genoese were decisively defeated by the Venetians at Chioggia, south of Venice.

DEBACLE ON THE DANUBE

Ottoman ascendancy in eastern Europe was conclusively demonstrated at Nicopolis on September 25, 1396, when the flower of European chivalry was overthrown by the previously underestimated Muslims. The defeat of the Christian army confirmed Turkish rule over the Balkans and put Hungary, the strongest Christian kingdom in the region, on the defensive.

The Christian forces comprised a Hungarian army under their king, Sigismund, and a large contingent of knights from western Europe, chiefly French, who had been rallied by the duke of Burgundy to throw the Ottomans out of Europe. Outside the walls of the Ottoman stronghold of Nicopolis on the Danube River, the frontier between Ottoman and Hungarian territory, the Hungarians and Western knights joined up with the fleet of the Knights Hospitalers, which had sailed up the Danube from the Black Sea. The French, led by the duke of Burgundy's twenty-four-year-old son, were experienced and superbly equipped, but overconfidence led them to relax their vigilance, and the arrival of the main Ottoman army caught them by surprise.

Sigismund counseled caution, but the French insisted on plunging into the attack. At first this policy seemed justified. The

French cavalry charged uphill toward the Ottoman army, which was drawn up across the road to the Bulgarian capital, Tirnovo; the heavily armored French swept aside the light Turkish irregular horsemen. Though thrown from their horses or forced to dismount by lines of pointed stakes driven into the ground, the French routed the Ottomans and again drove off the enemy light cavalry. Believing the battle won, they pursued their foes without pausing to rest.

But they had been lured into a trap. Nearing the top of the hill, they saw to their horror the main body of Ottoman cavalry emerge at a gallop over the crest. Disheartened and exhausted by the heat and dust, the French fought desperately; however, they had no choice but to surrender.

The victorious Ottomans and their Serbian allies then fought a second battle by the Danube against the Hungarians; this encounter resulted in another defeat for the Christians. Many of Sigismund's troops fled across the river, and the king himself escaped by ship, but losses on both sides were great. After the battle, 3,000 captive Christians were killed by order of the Ottoman sultan, Bajazet, although he spared many of the French nobles for the ransoms that would be paid for their release.

declared their honor slighted and, refusing even to wait until the size and formation of the Ottoman army had been assessed, insisted that they should lead the attack.

And so while Sigismund waited in the rear, the Western knights, the most illustrious soldiers of Christendom, charged wildly up the hill toward the enemy. "Think of the folly, and the pity of it!" lamented the French chronicler Froissart. "If they had only waited for the king of Hungary, who had at least 16,000 men, they could have done great deeds; but pride was their downfall." Scattering a screen of light Turkish cavalry, the knights found themselves checked by a line of stakes whose sharpened points were at the height of a horse's belly. They continued their advance on foot, pulling out the stakes as they went, until they engaged with the Ottomans' forward infantry units. After routing these, the Crusaders pressed on, imagining that the day was already theirs. But on reaching the summit of the hill, they were confronted by Bajazet's main army of janissaries and sipahis. Then "his hosts and chariots came against them in battle array, like the moon when she is new," a chronicler recorded. Dismounted and burdened by their armor, the Crusaders were flung back in disarray and all but annihilated. John of Nevers was one of the few French knights to escape slaughter, being preserved for the ransom he would fetch.

Dismayed by the sight of the riderless horses of the Western knights plunging back into their camp, Sigismund's vassals and allies fled across the river. The king and his Hungarian troops gallantly entered the fray, but then the Serbian cavalry of Stephen Lazarevich came to the aid of the Ottomans, and the Hungarians were driven back. Sigismund was ferried by fishing boat to the allied fleet and made his escape down the Danube. Most of his troops were left to face the bloody rage of Bajazet, who ordered the slaughter of every man over twenty until his own counselors, sick of the carnage, prevailed on him to stop.

Some of those who survived were later paraded before King Sigismund as he sailed through the Dardanelles. The Ottomans "led us to the sea," reported one of the captives, "and one after the other they abused the king of Hungary as he passed, and mocked him and called him to come out of the boat and deliver his people: And this they did to make fun of him, and skirmished a long time with each other on the sea. But they did not do him any harm, and so he went away."

Thus ended the Christian challenge to the Ottoman advance. The bravery of both the Western knights and the Hungarian troops had been beyond question, and if only they had fought as a combined army with a prudent strategy, the result of the battle could well have been different. "We lost the day by the pride and vanity of these French," concluded Sigismund. "If they had believed my advice, we had enough men to fight our enemies."

Once the Crusader menace was removed, Bajazet resumed the siege of Constantinople, intending to press it to a full-scale assault. Penned behind their walls, unable to work their fields outside the city, the inhabitants survived only because the Ottomans lacked the naval forces that would have prevented food convoys from getting through. Many died, though, and others surrendered to the Turks.

Manuel prayed constantly for relief: "Lord Jesus Christ, let it not come about that the great multitude of Christian peoples should hear it said that it was during the days of the emperor Manuel that the city, with all its holy and venerable monuments of the faith, was delivered to the infidel." He also sent pleas for help to all the crowned heads of Europe. Again only the French court offered practical support, sending a small force under Marshal Boucicaut, one of the survivors of Nicopolis, who inflicted several minor defeats on Ottoman forces in 1399. But Boucicaut knew that a much greater effort was needed if Constantinople was to be saved, and he persuaded Manuel to go and argue his case in person before the rulers of western Europe. In December 1399, the emperor set out, beginning a three-year round of the Italian, French, and English courts that brought him much sympathy and precious little else.

While he was away, Bajazet prepared to administer the final blow to Constantinople. By 1402, after eight years' siege, the city was on the point of collapse. Every day more of its inhabitants left the shelter of its walls to give themselves up; the small French contingent left by Boucicaut could not find enough food in the city and had to provision themselves by raiding outside its walls. Bajazet was so confident that the city would soon be in his hands that he had begun allotting its great buildings to his officers, reserving the church of Saint Sophia for his own use as a palace. But at the eleventh hour, his ambitions were thwarted. Bajazet lifted his blockade; all troops in Europe were rushed to Asia. A new and terrible conqueror was advancing into Anatolia from the east.

The name of this dreadful foe was Tamerlane. Styling himself "the scourge of God" and campaigning with legendary ferocity, he had carved out the vast Mongol Empire in central Asia in the last three decades of the fourteenth century, and in the summer of 1402, he was to overwhelm the Ottomans at Ankara in Anatolia. Bajazet's defeat was largely due to his failure to establish his absolute authority over the Anatolian principalities, whose loyalty did not survive the test of battle. Bajazet himself was to die in captivity in Anatolia, and in the following ten years, a good number of the newly conquered territories regained their independence while Bajazet's sons waged a futile civil war.

This reverse, however, was to prove only a temporary check to the advance of the Ottomans, whose greatest days were yet to come. In 1453, they finally succeeded in capturing Constantinople and proceeded to reestablish their rule in the Balkan and Anatolian provinces. At its peak in the mid-sixteenth century under Sulayman the Magnificent, the empire comprised—in addition to the Balkans and Anatolia—Hungary, the Crimea, Mesopotamia, Syria, Egypt, and most of North Africa. Constantinople—into which the first Ottoman settlers had entered during the reign of Bajazet in the fourteenth century—was to remain the seat of the Ottoman sultanate for five centuries.

THE FURY OF THE STEPPES

3 "I am the scourge of God appointed to chastise you, since no one knows the remedy for your iniquity except me. You are wicked, but I am more wicked than you, so be silent!" Thus spoke the all-powerful Mongol conqueror Tamerlane to a delegation of citizens outside the gates of Damascus, the greatest city in Syria, in early 1401. The citizens had come to protest that the tribute demanded of them was beyond their means, but Tamerlane's words persuaded them otherwise. Even after they had paid up, however, Tamerlane's wrath was not appeased, and he handed over the city to his rapacious soldiers. What happened next to the hapless citizens was described by the historian ibn-Taghribirdi, son of one of the Syrian generals: "They were bastinadoed, crushed in presses, scorched in flames, and suspended head down; their nostrils were stopped with rags full of fine dust, which they inhaled each time they took a breath so that they almost died."

Characteristically, after setting fire to the ransacked city, Tamerlane withdrew his army from Syria and marched on toward his next target. This pattern of ruthless and apparently purposeless destruction had been continually repeated for more than three decades, and by the time of his death in 1405, Tamerlane had amassed an empire in central Asia that included Transoxiana, Afghanistan, Persia, and Iraq; he had also sacked the cities of Sarai in Russia and Delhi in India and had defeated the armies of his two main rival empire builders, the Turkish Ottomans and the Egyptian Mamluks. The fact that this empire was held together almost entirely by Tamerlane's own force of will, and that it fell apart very soon after his death, was of little comfort to his victims, who died by the hundreds of thousands. Indeed, Tamerlane's ingenious ways of putting his enemies to death contributed to his success: The mere rumor of his approach was enough to strike terror into the hearts of a hostile army or a beleaguered town, and the pyramids of skulls that Tamerlane erected outside the walls of the cities he sacked advised all who passed of the futility of rebellion.

But although Tamerlane often behaved with unparalleled cruelty and was certainly illiterate, he was hardly a simple barbarian. Both his followers and his enemies agreed that he was a highly intelligent man. He was a sincere and practicing Muslim who had a passion for debating with religious scholars and philosophers such testing matters as the nature of martyrdom, the legitimacy of making war on fellow Muslims, and the correct way of reading the Koran, the holy book of Islam. Contemporary reports of these debates show Tamerlane employing an incisive style of thinking and speaking that betokened a genuine thirst for knowledge. He hated deception of all kinds, especially self-deception. *Rasti Rusti*—"Truth is safety"—was the Persian motto on his signet ring.

The diverse elements in Tamerlane's character—cruelty and savagery on the one hand, piety and intelligence on the other—reflected the complex makeup of the

Seated on a cushioned throne in front of his tent, the Mongol conqueror Timur the Lame, known in the West as Tamerlane, holds an audience while his servants look on. This detail from an early-fifteenth-century miniature included in a history of his conquests is an idealized portrait and does not reveal the permanent injuries to his right leg and arm that he received during a skirmish as a young man, but the Mongolian features, spare frame, and beard are probably true to life. Tamerlane's tactical skills as well as his ferocity and courage in battle made him the most feared warrior of his time.

world into which he was born. He spoke Turkish and Persian but was by descent a Mongol—that is, a member of the nomadic Asian people whose conquests under Genghis Khan in the early thirteenth century stretched from the Yellow Sea in the east to the Danube in the west. After the death of Genghis Khan in 1227, the vast Mongol Empire had continued to expand under his descendants: China and the Mongolian heartland were ruled by the dynasty of the great khan, Russia by the khan of the Golden Horde, Persia by the Ilkhan dynasty, and Transoxiana and Turkestan in central Asia by the Chagatai khan. Relationships among these dynasties fluctuated between uneasy alliance and outright hostility, and in the early fourteenth century, one section of the Chagatai khanate broke away to form the separate khanate of

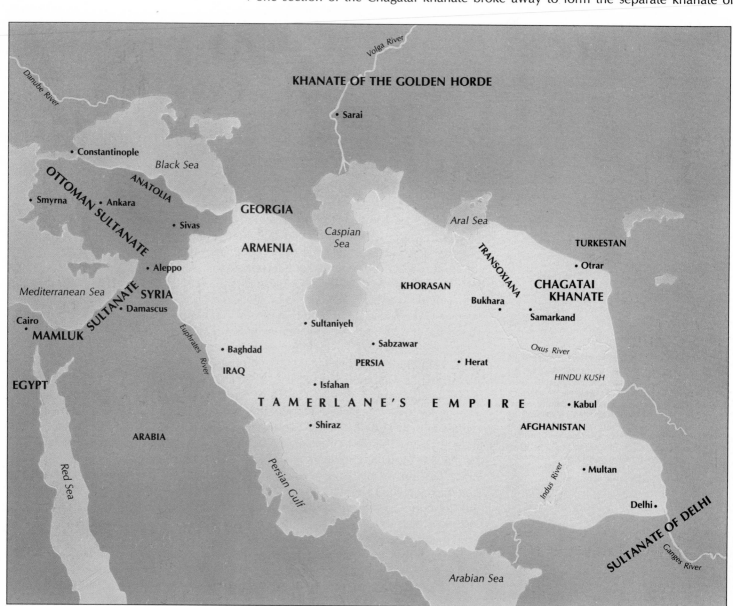

Mughalistan in the region of Turkestan. To the west of the Mongols, between Asia and Europe, two separate Muslim empires—the Ottoman sultanate of Turkey and the Mamluk sultanate of Egypt and Syria—were vigorously expanding. And to the south there flourished a third Muslim empire, the Delhi sultanate of northern India.

Tamerlane belonged to the loose confederacy of Mongol tribes who took their name from Genghis Khan's second son, the founder of the Chagatai dynasty. In China and Persia, the Mongols had come to terms with the customs of the indigenous peoples and the demands of settled life, but the Chagatai tribes of Transoxiana gloried in the traditional ways of the steppe nomad that had prevailed in the days of Genghis Khan. The Spanish diplomat Ruy González de Clavijo, who went on an embassy to Tamerlane in 1402, described their way of life. "These Chagatais with whom we are guests were nomad folk living in tents and booths, for indeed they possess no other permanent habitation, both summer and winter living in the open." In the summer they planted crops in the plains. In the winter, after the crops had been harvested, they migrated to warmer lands farther south. "Thus do they all spend their lives: for these people possess great herds, namely of camels, horses, and sheep but of cows only a few." The Chagatai spent their lives in the saddle, and in times of war, the Chagatai army was the Chagatai on the move: men, women, children, and livestock. The children learned to ride almost before they could walk and were usually accomplished archers by early adolescence. It was not unknown for the women to fight, and Western reports of Mongol female warriors came to be elaborated into fanciful legends of Amazon armies on the Eastern steppes.

Despite their notorious resistance to change, in the course of the thirteenth century, many of the Chagatai had, formally at least, abandoned the old Mongol shamanist paganism and become Muslims. Throughout his life, however, Tamerlane's own version of Islam was complicated by his attachment to the rites of his Mongol forebears, as well as by his fascinated devotion to mysticism and astrology. In particular, he was a devotee of the quasi-occult medieval science of physiognomy. Part divination, part detective work, physiognomy is the art of deducing the inner character of people or of things from external appearances. Archbishop John of Sultaniyeh, a Catholic envoy residing in Persia, reported that Tamerlane "says he knows the thoughts and cogitations of men; these are revealed to him by an angel. That is why no one dare plot against him."

The two main towns of Chagatid Transoxiana were Samarkand and Bukhara. The oasis town of Samarkand had, until the early thirteenth century, been the chief Muslim city in central Asia. It was a point of convergence for the camel trains of merchandise coming and going between China and the Muslim world; it was also a center of Muslim scholarship, famous for its madrasas (religious teaching colleges). Then Genghis Khan's Mongols had sacked the town in 1220 and massacred most of the population. In the early fourteenth century, the place seemed destined to linger on as a decaying backwater.

Tamerlane, the son of a shepherd, was born around 1336 at Qais, about fifty miles south of Samarkand. He was named Timur, meaning "Iron" in Turkish. It is impossible to be sure about much concerning his early years, for medieval chroniclers grafted tales of omens and predictions onto accounts of his life. At some time in his youth, however, he began to combine his career as shepherd with that of sheep stealer; it was not uncommon for Chagatai tribes to supplement their incomes by rustling and warfare. Ibn-Arabshah, an Arab scholar who was captured by Tamerlane

During the last three decades of the fourteenth century, Tamerlane conquered an empire that stretched from central Asia almost to the Mediterranean. His base was the Chagatai Khanate, one of four divisions of the thirteenth-century Mongol Empire after the death of its founder, Genghis Khan. Tamerlane never held the office of khan, which was reserved for direct descendants of Genghis; however, as military commander, his name appeared alongside that of the khan on state currency, including the silver coin shown above. In a series of lightning campaigns, he defeated the Egyptian Mamluks in Syria and the Turkish Ottomans at Ankara in Anatolia. He overwhelmed the rival Mongol khanate of the Golden Horde and put its capital to the sword; and he invaded northern India and devastated the lands of its rulers, the Delhi sultans. Lacking a stable administrative system, the empire he created did not long survive his death; but the labors of artists and artisans from the lands he conquered ensured that the Chagatai capital endured as a monument of Islamic arts and sciences.

This panorama, probably painted in Turkestan in central Asia in the early fifteenth century, depicts everyday life in a nomad camp. While horses graze and dogs gambol, clothes are washed and wrung out and a meal is cooked over a fire; the richly clad personage at right prepares his saddle for a hunting trip, on which he will take the weapons hung from a tripod of sticks behind him. Contemptuous of city life, Tamerlane's soldiers retained the nomadic customs of their Mongol ancestors. Unlike most other Muslim peoples, who fought only against the infidel, they were almost constantly on the move, in search of new pastures for their animals and new cities to plunder for booty.

in Damascus and later wrote a hostile biography, thought that it was during a sheep-stealing foray that he acquired the wound and the limp that led him to be called Timur-i-Lenk, or Timur the Lame, anglicized as Tamerlane or Tamburlaine.

In the politically chaotic conditions that then prevailed in the steppe and desert of Transoxiana, leadership was not something that could be inherited or bought; it had to be fought for and maintained by courage and military prowess, which Tamerlane had in abundance. His early successes as a bandit put him at the head of a small group of followers who were bound to him by ties of personal allegiance. Intelligent and fearless, he would lead his armies from the front throughout his life. Slowly his gang of rustlers expanded into a warband, and by 1361, he was recognized as the

leader of the Barlas tribe of Chagatai Mongols. In the course of the next ten years, by a mixture of military force and cunning diplomacy, making and breaking alliances with neighboring tribal chieftains according to the needs of the moment, Tamerlane made himself master of all the Chagatai khanate of Transoxiana.

Nevertheless, Tamerlane could not assume the formal title of khan. The ruler of the Chagatai had to be a descendant of Genghis Khan, and Tamerlane and his fellow warriors had too much reverence for this tradition to ignore it. Tamerlane therefore pretended to govern the empire in the name of Suyurghatmish, an undistinguished and very young descendant of Genghis Khan. The boy puppet in Samarkand was given the title of khan, while his real master, Tamerlane, remained content with the simple title emir (commander).

His power base established, Tamerlane was ready to fulfill his destiny. Although he could not claim the revered world conqueror Genghis Khan as his ancestor, two of his wives—and he had the four permitted by Islamic law—were directly descended from Genghis; it is also apparent that Tamerlane considered himself Genghis's spiritual heir and that he consciously modeled his exploits on those of his terrible predecessor. As well as boasting that he was "the Scourge of God," sent to punish people for their sins, he styled himself Sahib al-Qiran, or "Master of the Fortunate Conjunction"—that is, of the astrologically auspicious conjunction of Mars, Jupiter, and Saturn. Tamerlane believed that he was predestined to rule the world. This had been decreed by God and was written in the stars.

In the course of the next thirty-five years, Tamerlane's army was to campaign in Mughalistan, Afghanistan, Persia, Iraq, the Caucasus, the Russian steppes, India, Syria, and Turkey. The relentless yet almost haphazard trajectory of these campaigns was largely determined by the nature of the army itself. In assuming leadership of the Chagatai horde, Tamerlane had mounted a tiger from which it would be dangerous to dismount. If he lost a battle or was seen to lose his grip, then his Chagatai warriors might turn upon him, depose him, and murder him. Therefore, the Chagatai had to be kept on the move almost continuously and promised new kingdoms to conquer, new cities to plunder.

Other factors behind the constant movement were the expense of maintaining a large standing army and the quest for new pasturage. In order to pay for the army, massively profitable pillaging expeditions were undertaken; in order to assure the success of these predatory expeditions, a large military force had to be kept permanently on the move. And besides the string of horses that each warrior brought with him on campaign, there was also a vast train of pack animals carrying supplies and munitions. It was impossible to keep the whole army stationary for any length of time. Either the whole army must move on or the force must split up and go off in different directions. The troops were usually fed by requisitioning supplies from the local populace, a system of catering that hardly differed from organized plunder.

In choosing a particular target for his voracious army, however, Tamerlane usually had a clear goal in mind. Often the motive was economic: He wished to assure the security of a trade route, to protect a merchant community from the depredations of warlord brigands, or to avenge the mistreatment that merchants from his lands had received in foreign parts. And the terror that he visited upon his enemies was not wholly indiscriminate: After a city had yielded to his army, he took care to protect the scholars and intellectuals from his marauding soldiers, and he sent back the

A PERSIAN HISTORY OF THE WORLD

Tamerlane's Mongol predecessors as rulers of Persia were the Ilkhans, generous patrons of the arts who made their capital, Tabriz, a flourishing cultural center. In the field of scholarship, one of their most ambitious ventures was to commission a history of the world, produced under the supervision of the vizier, or chief minister, Rashid al-Din.

Scholars from all over the world were summoned to assist on the monumental work, which included sections on the Turks, the Chinese, the Europeans, the Jews, and the Indians, as well as accounts of the ancient kings of Persia and the rise of Islam. The diverse origins of the artists employed to illustrate the manuscript are displayed in the miniatures shown here, which reveal a mixture of Persian, Mongol, Chinese, and Byzantine Christian influences.

Disgorged from the belly of a gigantic fish, the prophet Jonah rests in the shade of a gourd plant that has sprung forth miraculously to provide him with food and shade. Many of the stories recounted in the Old Testament form part of the sacred literature of Islam as well as of Christianity.

2 The fourth-century-BC Greek conqueror Alexander the Great, here clad in fourteenth-century Mongol armor, leads his troops toward the fog-enshrouded regions of the north. Painted in Chinese style, the swirling, silver-lined clouds cause consternation even to the horses, who exchange a look of despair.

3 An angel emerges from a cloud to anoint the young Muhammad, future founder of Islam. Muhammad is said to have accompanied his uncle on trading journeys to Syria; this scene records the occasion when the boy was recognized by a Syrian monk—shown here in the tower at right—as a prophet whose coming was predicted in the Scriptures.

4 Mahmud of Ghazni, who in the eleventh century founded a Muslim empire that was to stretch from northern Persia to the Ganges basin in India, stands on a platform before his throne. He is donning a robe of honor presented by the caliph of Baghdad, the spiritual leader of Islam.

captured artisans—metalworkers, stonemasons, armorers—to work on the buildings and in the munitions factories of Samarkand.

During the 1370s, Tamerlane concerned himself with securing his homeland around Samarkand and extending his rule by campaigns against the Mughals of Turkestan to the east and the peoples of Khorasan to the west. These were mostly punitive campaigns, in which Tamerlane used his forces to protect the cities and agriculture of Transoxiana from the raiding of other nomadic tribes. But at the same time, he was developing his army, the tool with which he intended to expand his empire in the west by occupying the settled regions of Persia and Afghanistan.

The fourteenth century was preeminently the age of the cavalry warrior in both Asia and Europe, and indeed, cavalry formed the most important part of Tamerlane's army. The Chagatai warriors, however, unlike Western feudal knights, were not accustomed to the heavy lance. Instead, like their Mongol predecessors, they relied on their skills as cavalry archers. The traditional Mongol bow, made from layers of sinew and horn and curved forward at the tips where the string was attached, could fire off arrows that traveled farther and had more penetrating power than even the famous English longbow. Moreover, this bow was compact enough to be managed with ease and speed from the saddle. The Chagatai warrior also carried a sword and was lightly armored—the small steppe horses could hardly have borne the weight of a man clad in heavy plate armor of the sort that was coming into fashion in Europe.

A notable feature in the training of these warriors was the Great Hunt, an exercise in mass coordination and individual courage. The entire army, organized in its battlefield formations, would encircle a designated area of the Transoxiana plain. Then, stage by stage, the circle was tightened, driving the wolves and other wild animals caught within its compass toward the center. Only when the ring was closed tight and the signal given were the soldiers allowed to use their javelins and arrows to kill the maddened beasts.

Although Chagatai cavalry furnished the elite shock troop of the army, the total was swelled by a vast number of auxiliaries. Bertrando de Mignanelli, an Italian merchant residing in Syria at the time of Tamerlane's invasion of that country in 1400, reckoned that the cavalry warriors made up only about one-tenth of an estimated total strength of 300,000. The remainder of the army consisted of an enormous number of attendant "laborers, stonecutters, shoemakers, charioteers, carpenters, wall builders, artisans, cooks, millers, and others who did manual labor." And in addition to the visible army, there was an invisible army of spies. Tamerlane attached great importance to espionage, and wandering dervishes and merchants traveled backward and forward across Asia collecting information for him.

The army was organized in descending units of 10. A force of 10,000 was called a *tuman;* it was divided into sections of 1,000 under more junior officers, and those sections in turn had subalterns commanding sections of 100. It was an efficient way of organizing the troops; it was also a politically motivated device, for Tamerlane aimed to use army discipline in such a way as to crosscut old tribal loyalties and weaken Chagatai groups who might one day turn against him. Not only was each tuman usually composed of people from a mixture of tribes, but the senior commands in this army were held mostly by those who owed their high rank to Tamerlane's personal favor. The old Chagatai chieftains who might have plotted against Tamerlane were usually excluded from positions of command that could be converted into independent power bases.

Although Tamerlane found the Chagatai difficult to control in peacetime, they were disciplined on the battlefield, where trumpets and banners were used to direct their movements. The responses of the various sections of the army—vanguard, left wing, right wing, center—allowed a degree of tactical planning by their commander. Like other military leaders of the time, Tamerlane used the game of chess as an aid to working out his battle tactics. Tamerlane, however, found ordinary chess too limiting, so he played an expanded game on a larger board with extra pieces such as camels, giraffes, sentinels, war engines, and a vizier. Tamerlane's son and successor, Shah Rukh, is said to have been so named because Tamerlane happened to be moving the *rukh,* or rook, on the chessboard when news of the birth was announced to him.

In 1381, this massive force entered Persia for the first time. Persia had been occupied by the Mongols in the mid-thirteenth century, but since the death of the last effective ruler of the Ilkhan dynasty in 1335, the region had been divided among quarreling local regimes. The most curious of these successor states was centered in the town of Sabzawar, in the north of Persia, where the mysterious Sarbadars—who took their name from the Persian words for "head on a gibbet"—had established an independent republic ruled by a governor instead of a hereditary dynasty. Sabzawar surrendered to Tamerlane readily enough, but the tribal rulers in the provinces to the south of the Caspian Sea offered more stubborn resistance, and Persia as a whole proved difficult to occupy permanently. A number of the cities found that the burden of taxation imposed on them by the occupying Chagatai administration did not differ significantly from organized pillage, and they adopted a foolhardy policy of rebellion.

After crushing a revolt in Isfizar in 1383, Tamerlane cemented 2,000 captives, still living, inside the walls of a tower. For hours their screams and moans floated through the desolate streets and orchards of Isfizar. Four years later, the citizens of Isfahan in southern Persia rebelled and killed the tax collectors and agents that Tamerlane had left there. Tamerlane's Arab biographer, ibn-Arabshah, described the consequence: "Timur perceived that evil crime; and Satan puffed up his nostrils and he forthwith moved his camp and drew the sword of his wrath and took arrows from the quiver of his tyranny and advanced to the city, roaring and overthrowing, like a dog, or lion, or leopard." Tamerlane suppressed the rebellion with ease and took his revenge in characteristic fashion. He posted guards at the doors of the scholars and teachers of religion to protect them and their families. Then he sent the rest of his army into the city, commanding each soldier to return with the head of an Isfahani. Thus Tamerlane "loosened the reins of the cutting sword in the fields of their necks and made their graves in the bellies of wolves and hyenas and crops of birds." Ibn-Arabshah also described how some of the surviving small children were gathered on a hill in the hope that Tamerlane might be moved to pity and would order the massacre to cease. Tamerlane and his retinue rode over the children as if they had not seen them. After the massacre was over and tens of thousands of the Isfahanis slaughtered, pyramids of skulls were erected around the perimeter of the town. Such towers of skulls served as advertisements to the traveler, warning him that he was journeying through Tamerlane's empire of terror.

Writing twenty years after Tamerlane's death, a historian employed by one of his grandsons was to claim that such atrocities were unfortunate but necessary parts of the conqueror's strategy. Tamerlane's "generous personality manifested the boundless grace of God," insisted Sharaf al-Din Yazdi, "while the purest virtue and philanthropy were concealed in his light-seeking mind; and such acts of wrath and

امیر حاجی سیف الدین از نیرو
اقبال صاحبقران نصرت فرّ
پیش از همه شمشیر کشید
حمله کرد و دست چپ دشمن
که در مقابل او بود زهم شکست
و برآمد بینند
چنان برکنند لشکر یا
که پنا یا مد همی شر پای
چند قوشون که از سپاه دشمن یا
آمد بود در وان شدند که آن
عتبه گاه امیر حاجی سیف الدین
در آیند جهانشاه بهادر چون
این حال مشاهده کرد با سپاه
خود پیش ایشان رفته بزخم
شمشیر آبدار و ضرب سنان آتش

Mounted on an armored horse and shaded by a parasol, Tamerlane is shown directing his followers into battle with his whip in this double-page miniature from the early fifteenth century. Slung at his hip are a Mongol bow and a curved sword, weapons in whose use the Chagatai troops were trained from childhood. Cavalry—represented here by two horsemen leaping toward enemy archers— were the main strike force of Tamerlane's army in open battles; the infantry, here waiting in reserve in the shelter of a hill, were more valuable in sieges.

retribution as were ostensibly committed in the initial stages of his campaigns by some of his followers and partisans were prompted only by the exigencies of conquest and the necessities of world empire.'' Certainly this was a cruel age, and similar atrocities were committed by Tamerlane's enemies as well as by armies in Europe. Nor was Tamerlane the inventor of the pyramid of skulls: Genghis Khan before him had made use of these grandiose memento mori. Perhaps Tamerlane was deliberately modeling himself on Genghis Khan and using atrocity to link himself in the minds of his contemporaries with his bloody predecessor. In addition, of course, the massacres served as a deterrent: Other Persian cities thought twice before attempting to follow the example of Isfahan.

A month after the massacre at Isfahan, Tamerlane was at Shiraz, which submitted to him without a fight. Dawlatshah, the medieval biographer of Persian poets, reported that Tamerlane showed especial eagerness to meet the town's most famous citizen, Hafiz, the greatest poet of Persia. Hafiz's fame rested on his quatrains, which espoused both the sensual joys of love and wine and the mystical doctrines of the Sufis, who held that direct, personal experience of God was of more importance than the elaborate disciplines of conventional Islam. Tamerlane was devoted to Sufism and fond of poetry. However, according to Dawlatshah, he had a bone to pick with Hafiz. Hafiz had previously written the following couplet about a Turkish girl: ''If that

unkindly Shiraz Turk would take my heart within her hand, / I'd give Bukhara for the mole upon her cheek, or Samarkand."

The irate Tamerlane pointed out that he had expended a great deal of time, effort, and blood in order to secure and embellish those two cities, yet here was the wretched poet proposing to give them away for a spot on a girl's cheek! Hafiz, always quick-witted, replied that it was through such excessive generosity that he had fallen on hard times. Tamerlane was delighted and dismissed the poet with a present.

Sultaniyeh, in northwest Persia, a former capital of the old Ilkhans, was occupied by Tamerlane in 1384, and thereafter it served as a regional capital and operations base for campaigns farther north and west. It was also the place where Tamerlane's wives and children were left for safety during those campaigns. The chief of his wives was Saray-Mulk-Khanum, a descendant of Genghis Khan. Little is known about Tamerlane's relationship with her, although certainly she was afforded the respect due to the consort of a great man. When Clavijo, the Spanish ambassador, recorded seeing Saray-Mulk-Khanum in Samarkand, the lady was surrounded by 300 attendants, was wearing a veil, and had apparently painted her face with white lead so that she looked as if she was wearing a paper mask.

The period from 1392 to 1396 was to become known as the Five Years' Campaign. During these years, Tamerlane's armies marched and countermarched through the mountains of the Caucasus and the Hindu Kush, the deserts of Persia, and the steppelands of south Russia. The little Christian kingdom of Georgia, a favorite target of Tamerlane's armies, was invaded and pillaged a minimum of six times. It was prosperous and fertile, at first at least, and if there was any danger of the Chagatai resting in idle discontent, they could always be sent to plunder this underdefended region. Also, since this was almost the only region in which Tamerlane's army was engaged against Christians rather than fellow Muslims, his court propagandists seized the opportunity to portray Tamerlane as a ghazi, a warrior fighting for the Islamic faith.

The Five Years' Campaign was crowned in 1395 by victory over the rival Mongol Empire of the Golden Horde in the south Russian steppeland and the utter destruction of the Golden Horde's capital at Sarai on the Volga. As a result of the devastation in the region, merchant wagon trains from the east that had previously proceeded north of the Caspian on their way to ports of the Black Sea now found it easier and safer to travel through Tamerlane's lands south of the Caspian and pay their tolls to his collectors. The steppeland around Sarai was left to the camel and the antelope.

The vast bronze cauldron at left and above—more than eight feet in diameter and almost as tall as a standing man—bears the name and titles of Tamerlane amid floral arabesque decorations. Cast by Persian artisans, it was commissioned in 1399 by the Mongol leader for the shrine of a Sufi holy man in Turkestan, where it probably stood in the center of a courtyard in place of a fountain or pool. Sufi divines, whose mystical doctrines often differed from orthodox Islam, were held in high regard by Tamerlane and inspired many acts of piety.

Returned to Samarkand, Tamerlane devoted himself to the adornment of his capital. Spacious gardens were laid out and palaces constructed; abundant quantities of marble, porcelain, gold, silk, and precious stones were employed in their decoration. All these works, however, were intended not for Tamerlane's personal enjoyment but to impress future generations with his magnificence, and after two years—the longest interval between campaigns in his career—he began to weary of the arts of peace.

In the spring of 1398, Tamerlane's army crossed the mountains of the Hindu Kush and entered Afghanistan. This was first and foremost an expedition to secure booty, and its goal was Delhi, the capital of the Delhi sultanate in northern India. Founded in the early thirteenth century, this dynasty had reached its peak in the mid-fourteenth century but was now in decline; many of the provinces under its control had asserted their independence, civil war had raged for three years from 1394, and the present emperor, Mahmud, was a mere puppet in the hands of his vizier.

During its passage over the Hindu Kush, the army found its way impeded not only by snow and ice but also by the guerrilla warfare of the wild and primitive Kafir tribesmen. In Kabul, Tamerlane rested the main part of his army, and not until September did he reach the Indus River. Although few of the Muslim and Hindu principalities in northern India were prepared to unite against the invader, some were nevertheless capable of resisting fiercely, and the city of Multan was besieged for six months before it fell to an advance contingent of the Chagatai army led by Tamer-

This reconstruction shows the imperial pavilion erected on the plain of Kani-Gil outside Samarkand to celebrate the weddings of five of Tamerlane's grandsons in 1404. Tamerlane had lived most of his life in tents rather than palaces, and for this occasion—held toward the end of his life, when his empire stretched to its farthest extent—he sought to impress his foreign guests with a supreme example of his tentmakers' art. The outside of the pavilion—which was reported to measure 100 paces square—was decorated with silks and velvet studded with gems; the inside was lined with brocaded tapestries and ermine and squirrel furs, and the floor was laid with rich carpets. Envoys from as far away as China and Constantinople, as well as from Tamerlane's subject domains, were housed in thousands of lesser tents surrounding the central marquee.

lane's grandson. Many of the Chagatai horses had been lost in the crossing of the Hindu Kush, and more had since died of disease and famine on the Indian plains. Tamerlane's troops were tired, but they were also at risk from the vast number of captives they had already taken in their advance to the Indus, reputedly as many as 100,000. Tamerlane decided to remove this risk by having the captives slaughtered. At last, in December, the army was on the move toward Delhi.

Mahmud's vizier decided that the army of the Delhi sultanate would encounter

Tamerlane outside the city. According to Tamerlane's chronicler Nizam al-Din Shami, the Indian forces comprised "10,000 horses, 20,000 fully armored foot, and 120 war elephants, surging like the ocean and trumpeting like thunder clouds, armored with structures placed upon their backs." Lances in the form of scimitars with poisoned tips were attached to the elephants' tusks. Archers fired arrows from the fortified howdahs. Soldiers carrying primitive fire-rocket launchers marched alongside the elephants.

The Chagatai had never faced war elephants before, and Tamerlane was sufficiently perturbed to order one of his holy men to offer up special prayers to Allah for help against this unfamiliar branch of military technology. At the same time, more practical measures were taken against them. Caltrops—metal balls with sharp protruding spikes—were scattered on the field to damage the elephants' feet. A trench was hurriedly dug to halt their advance. A chain of yoked buffaloes created another line of defense. Tamerlane's most effective ploy, however, was to send ahead of his main force a squadron of camels laden with bales of straw. As the camels approached the elephants, the straw was fired, and urged on from behind, the incendiary camels charged. The elephants panicked and fled.

Such was the panic that many of the fleeing Indians were crushed to death trying to force their way through the gates of Delhi. Sultan Mahmud and his vizier fled farther, abandoning their capital to its fate. At first it seemed that this would not be so terrible as that of Isfahan and other Persian cities. While the greater part of his army rested outside the walls, Tamerlane made a triumphal entry and sat in state to receive the submission of Indian princelings. Orchestras played, celebratory odes were read, the princes paid homage, and even the elephants that had been captured in battle were made to kneel in submission to their new master. Chagatai taxgatherers and sightseers wandered around the city. Soon, however, insults were passing between the occupying troops and the citizens of Delhi, who resented the imposition of taxes and the requisitioning of their food supplies. Scuffles broke out, and these skirmishes escalated into a full-blown rebellion. The main army was ordered in and Delhi was given over to sack.

Tamerlane's soldiers fell on the city with pent-up fury. The army had suffered greatly in the previous months' campaigning. Their captives, the human booty that they could have sold as slaves, had been slaughtered on the eve of the battle for Delhi. Now the troops expected recompense and revenge for their sufferings. The majority of the populace was killed or enslaved. The most fortunate of the citizens were the skilled artisans; Tamerlane as usual reserved them for himself, sending them back to work for him in Samarkand. After the sack of Delhi, the army crossed the Ganges River to do some more pillaging, but no attempt was made to occupy the Delhi sultanate permanently.

After his spectacular success in India, Tamerlane again returned to Samarkand, but he did not stay there long. Provoked by a hostile expedition into Armenia led by the son of Bajazet, the Ottoman sultan, Tamerlane determined that the time had come for him to challenge his two most formidable enemies in the west, the Ottomans of Turkey and the Mamluks of Egypt and Syria. Tamerlane was particularly interested in humbling Bajazet, who had attempted to forge an alliance with the Mamluks against him and who had further provoked Tamerlane by giving shelter to leaders from Persia and Iraq who opposed his rule. Worse, Bajazet and his allies had refused to grant protection to merchants from Tamerlane's lands who were traveling to Turkey, and

During the fourteenth century, the decoration of buildings across Persia and central Asia with mosaics became increasingly elaborate. The first detail here shows an early geometric design of two colors contrasted with unglazed terra cotta *(top, left)*; the other examples, which date from the early fifteenth century, represent the colorful apogee of the art.

the economic well-being of Tamerlane's empire depended on trade almost as much as on pillage and the profits of war.

Tamerlane's army reached Sivas in eastern Turkey in August 1400. The town held out for eighteen days before its garrison surrendered upon receiving a promise that their blood would not be shed. Tamerlane, however, chose to interpret the remark literally; he had them buried alive in an underground vault.

Tamerlane might have advanced farther into Turkey that year, but he decided instead to secure his southern flank by attacking Mamluk Syria first. He was encouraged in his decision by the knowledge that Barquq, the experienced and vigorous Mamluk sultan, had died in 1399; his son and successor, al-Nasir Faraj, was only ten years old, and although he had inherited a well-stocked treasury and a powerful war machine, he lacked his father's authority.

In the autumn of 1400, Tamerlane entered Syria, and in October, his army arrived before the walls of the northern town of Aleppo. The main Mamluk army, quartered in Egypt, was slow to mobilize. The Aleppan garrison was reinforced by troops from the other provinces of Syria, and it speaks much for their morale that they decided to give battle at once; they would have been better advised to wait behind the city walls for the arrival of the main Egyptian army under Faraj. By now Tamerlane was using war elephants in battle, and they had the same disconcerting effect on the Mamluks as they had previously had on the Chagatai in India. The Mamluk forces fought bravely—Tamerlane commended the courage of their generals—but in the end they were defeated, and Aleppo was stormed and sacked. According to the Mamluk historian ibn-Taghribirdi, corpses covered the ground like a carpet.

Tamerlane had defeated the provincial Syrian army. He never defeated the main Mamluk army from Egypt because it, having marched north as far as Damascus, fell apart before it could even offer him battle. The disintegration of the Mamluk forces was hastened by the fear that Tamerlane and the Chagatai inspired in advance of their coming, a fear intensified by Tamerlane's widespread distribution of astrological leaflets that appeared to predict his inevitable victory. The main reason for the paralysis of the Mamluk army, however, was political dissension: Faraj was nervous of the possibility of an officers' coup while he was away on campaign, and rather than lose Egypt, he turned back to Cairo, leaving the citizens of Damascus to their fate.

The prominent civilians in Damascus hastened to negotiate the surrender of their city to Tamerlane. The celebrated Arab historian ibn-Khaldun, author of a definitive history of Muslim North Africa, attached himself to the timid delegation that presented itself at Tamerlane's tent, and thus occurred the meeting between the greatest scholar and the greatest warrior of the Muslim world. Far more than a simple chronicler, ibn-Khaldun was one of the world's leading philosophers of history, and in his writings, he had sought to show how a cyclical pattern dominated the history of civilizations. According to ibn-Khaldun, as societies and their rulers become civilized over the generations, old bonds of solidarity are weakened and the societies become prey to vigorous nomads from outside. The nomads' bonds of solidarity are strong, and they are usually able to invade and conquer the decaying settled societies; then, as the nomads set up their own regime and become civilized, they in their turn become subject to the cyclical law of decline and fall.

Hoping to see history being made, ibn-Khaldun had accompanied Sultan Faraj and his army from Egypt. Now he had the opportunity to meet the great nomad leader who seemed to vindicate his theory perfectly. Ibn-Khaldun considered the Chagatai

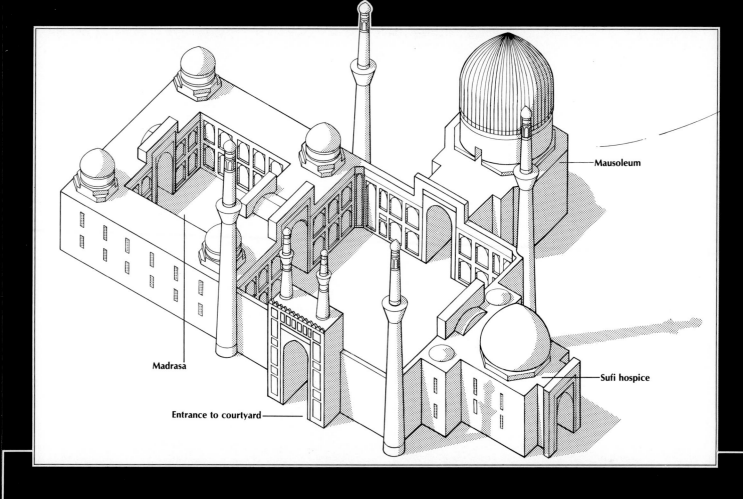

Mausoleum

Madrasa

Sufi hospice

Entrance to courtyard

A CONQUEROR'S LAST RESTING PLACE

The massive turquoise dome of the Gur-e Amir (Tomb of the Prince) dominates a religious complex in Tamerlane's capital of Samarkand. The other buildings—a Sufi hospice and a madrasa, or college for theological students, on opposite sides of a courtyard marked by four minarets—were built by Muhammad Sultan, Tamerlane's grandson and heir apparent; when Muhammad died at the age of twenty-nine in 1403,

Tamerlane ordered the construction of the mausoleum as a resting place for his body.

The twelve-foot-high dome consists of two shells, the top of the inner one being about forty feet lower than the outer. The inner dome, in addition to providing structural support, maintains the proportions of the interior of the chamber. All the exterior surfaces are decorated with mosaics.

Less than a year after the building was

completed, Tamerlane was dead. He was buried in the crypt, alongside his grandson; his cenotaph in the main chamber of the mausoleum was covered by a massive slab of dark, blue-green nephrite. During the customary funerary rites, the cries of mourning were accompanied by the beating of the conqueror's drum; its skin was slashed after the ceremony so that it might never sound again.

Blue and turquoise tiles emblazon the ribbed exterior of the dome of the Gur-e Amir. The interior of the inner dome *(below)* is ornamented with gilded papier-mâché, molded and carved in relief.

the purest of the Mongols, the ones who had stuck most closely to the fierce nomadic customs that had prevailed under Genghis Khan in the early thirteenth century.

As for Tamerlane, he was fond of historians—although they seem to have been less fond of him—and he had many questions he wanted to ask ibn-Khaldun. Over a series of meetings, he cross-questioned the philosopher-historian on a variety of topics. Where were the descendants of Nebuchadnezzar? To whom did the caliphate, the office of the spiritual leader of Islam, rightfully belong? Did ibn-Khaldun believe that he, Tamerlane, was destined to rule the world? Tamerlane also requested that ibn-Khaldun write him out a detailed report on the geography of North Africa (perhaps this might prove useful for some future campaign?) and pressed the historian to stay in his service. Ibn-Khaldun, however, had had enough; claiming that he was eager to fetch his family to join him, he secured a safe-conduct to leave Tamerlane's camp and slipped away, never to return.

Later, in a letter written to the ruler of Fez, he was to record his impressions of Tamerlane: "This king Timur is one of the greatest and mightiest of kings. Some attribute to him knowledge, others attribute to him heresy, still others attribute to him the employment of magic and sorcery, but in all this there is nothing; it is simply that he is highly intelligent and very perspicacious, addicted to debate and argumentation about what he knows and also about what he does not know."

The meeting between Tamerlane and the citizens of Damascus was less pleasant, and it ended in customary fashion with the sack of the city and general massacre. The Chagatai were by now very experienced at squeezing every last coin from their victims and at discovering every hidden treasure. Once again the master artisans—in Damascus, the glassblowers, metalworkers, and masons—were rounded up and sent to labor in captivity in Samarkand. Then Damascus was fired and Tamerlane's army began its retreat out of Syria. It is doubtful that Tamerlane had ever intended to occupy Syria permanently; the land could hardly provide sufficient pasturage over any length of time for the large army that Tamerlane had brought with him, and besides, his position was fast becoming untenable. A bold group of Mamluk officers had reoccupied Aleppo to his rear, and if the Ottoman sultan Bajazet should decide to move toward northern Syria, Tamerlane's forces would find themselves in a very precarious position.

The defeat of Bajazet was still Tamerlane's major goal. But again he delayed, choosing instead to invade Iraq and deal with the Jalayirid sultan of Baghdad. The Jalayirids were one of several dynasties that had succeeded the Ilkhans, and the sultan was an old ally of both the Mamluk and Ottoman sultanates. Baghdad was stormed by the Chagatai in July 1401, and each soldier was detailed to kill two male citizens and to bring back their heads. Such was the shortage of male citizens to slaughter that some of the Chagatai found themselves obliged to decapitate women and shave the women's heads in order to pass muster. Again, the intellectuals, artisans, and artists were spared the fate of their fellow citizens. In this case, the Jalayirid painters, deported from Baghdad to Samarkand, were to exercise a major influence on the future glorious development of the Timurid school of miniature painting.

The clash with Bajazet could be postponed no longer. In the summer of 1402, Tamerlane's army advanced into Turkish Anatolia and, evading Bajazet's attempt to intercept it, prepared to storm the provincial capital of Ankara. Siege preparations were abandoned, however, when Bajazet's army approached, and the two great

Muslim forces took up battle positions on the highland plains that extend to the north and the east of Ankara.

Bajazet, nicknamed Yilderim (the Thunderbolt) by his Turkish subjects, was perhaps the one Muslim leader who had no reason to fear Tamerlane. He had behind him a more or less unbroken string of victories against the Byzantines, Hungarians, Serbians, and rival Turkish dynasties, and in 1396, he had decisively defeated an army of European Crusaders at Nicopolis on the Danube. By these victories he had extended the rule of the Ottoman sultanate over all Bulgaria and Serbia and had completely surrounded Constantinople, the capital of the Christian empire of Byzantium. In his elite corps of janissaries, made up of handpicked Christian captives who had undergone rigorous training, Bajazet had a superbly disciplined and efficient fighting force. The single potential weakness of his army was the doubtful loyalty of some of his other troops: The small Turkish principalities in Anatolia had only recently been absorbed into Bajazet's empire, and the levies from these provinces were still reluctant to accept their new master.

In the event, the encounter between these two Muslim foes turned out to be as much a political revolt as a straightforward battle. Tamerlane's army had the advantage of being well rested, and it had secured the only important source of water near Ankara. But Bajazet's Anatolian troops, placed in the front line to absorb the brunt of the Chagatai first charge, crossed over to swell Tamerlane's forces before battle was joined and so sealed Bajazet's fate. Tamerlane's army still met with stiff opposition, in particular from Bajazet's janissaries and a contingent of Christian Serbians from the Balkans, but the desertion of the Anatolian levies proved decisive. Bajazet continued to fight almost to the last, wielding a heavy battle-ax to keep his attackers at bay. Only when it was absolutely clear that the day was lost did he attempt to ride off from the bloody field, but he was swiftly overtaken and made captive by the Chagatai horse archers.

According to some reports, Tamerlane kept his distinguished new captive in an iron cage, treating the once mighty Ottoman sultan like a beast in a menagerie. According to another account, Bajazet was forced to watch his favorite wife serve naked at Tamerlane's table. After eight months of enduring carefully staged humiliations, Bajazet died in captivity.

Tamerlane rewarded the deserters from Bajazet's army by reestablishing their independent principalities in eastern and central Anatolia. The mighty Ottoman Empire was plunged into civil war as Bajazet's four sons struggled among themselves for a decade. In the Byzantine capital of Constantinople, there was rejoicing at the news of Tamerlane's victory, for the city—which had been on the verge of surrendering to Bajazet in the summer of 1402—was now relieved from a six-year siege by the Ottoman army.

The Christian city of Smyrna on the Turkish coast was less fortunate. This port was held by the Knights Hospitalers, a military order of Christian knights, as a base for possible future Crusades against the Muslim occupiers of the Holy Land. During the sack of Smyrna by Tamerlane's army after a fifteen-day siege, a Christian fleet appeared on the horizon. To discourage the fleet from entering the harbor, Tamerlane had the severed heads of Smyrna's garrison collected and floated them out to sea on candlelit dishes, a macabre regatta.

Tamerlane returned to his beloved Samarkand in 1404. Although in practice the capital of Tamerlane's empire was wherever his army happened to be, Samarkand

Included in a personal horoscope cast in 1411 for Iskandar Sultan, a grandson of Tamerlane, this astrological chart depicts the positions of the stars and planets at the moment of the prince's birth in 1384. Inscribed in the inner circle are twelve roundels illustrated with signs of the zodiac; the planets are personified according to conventional tradition, Venus appearing as a woman playing a lute and Mars as a warrior holding a sword and a severed head. The four outer corners show Islamic angels bearing gifts. In the accompanying interpretive text, the court astrologer predicted for Iskandar— the ruler of Fars, in southwest Persia—good health, a long life, and victory in war. In fact, three years after this horoscope was cast, he rebelled unsuccessfully against his uncle Shah Rukh and was subsequently blinded and killed.

was the fixed center for the civilian officials who administered taxes and kept the imperial records. The city was now full of loot and of artisans laboring in bondage, and the Spanish diplomat Clavijo was impressed by its spaciousness and wealth. Surrounded by orchards and market gardens, the town contained gardens watered by conduits, many splendid houses, and a domed bazaar. Its population had been swollen by migrants from the surrounding provinces as well as by the captives taken during Tamerlane's campaigns, and many of the inhabitants were forced to sleep in the streets and gardens. The streets ran as narrow ravines between tall buildings so as to ensure the maximum amount of shade and coolness. On the western side of the city stood the old citadel of Gok-Saray where, said Clavijo, 1,000 or more captive workers were incarcerated, permanently engaged in making armor and munitions for Tamerlane's army.

Other workers were engaged in building the Gur-e Amir, a mausoleum constructed for Tamerlane's son that was eventually to contain the body of Tamerlane as well, and the vast cathedral mosque of Bibi Khanum, named for one of Tamerlane's wives. Tamerlane took a keen interest in the work. Finding the entrance porch of the mosque unimpressive, he ordered it to be demolished and rebuilt, and for good measure he had two of the architects responsible hanged, to encourage the others. Brought in a litter every morning to the site, he would urge on the workers by flinging portions of

meat down to them "as one would cast bones to dogs in a pit." When the work was going well, money replaced meat.

Tamerlane was now almost seventy years old. Clavijo reported that, when he was presented to the emperor, he had to stand very close, "for his sight was no longer good, indeed, he was so infirm and old that his eyelids were falling over his eyes and he could barely raise them to see." Even now, however, Samarkand could not hold Tamerlane for long. In the autumn of 1404, he began to plan his most ambitious campaign of all, the invasion of China. The Yuan dynasty, founded by Kublai Khan, a grandson of Genghis Khan, in 1272, had been overturned and replaced by the Ming in 1368. It is possible that Tamerlane, having crushed his enemies in the west by invading China, intended to restore the world empire of his Mongol forebears.

More immediately, preparations were made for a great imperial festival. This week-long celebration, held on the plain of Kani-Gil outside Samarkand, was in honor of the marriages of five of Tamerlane's grandsons; all the Chagatai chieftains attended, as well as envoys from Byzantium, Egypt, Syria, India, Mongolia, and China, each of whom arrived with lavish gifts. According to Clavijo, more than 20,000 tents were pitched on the plain around Tamerlane's own pavilions. There were performances by singers, instrumentalists, wrestlers, clowns, acrobats, and tightrope walkers; in ritual games, girls dressed as goats with golden horns were chased by skinners and tanners dressed as lions, leopards, and tigers.

A carved wooden box and two ewers, one of brass inlaid with silver and the other of white jade, bear witness to the fine handiwork that flourished under the patronage of Tamerlane's successors in the early fifteenth century. The variety of the arts practiced—painting, pottery, bookbinding, and weaving, as well as woodcarving and metalwork—reflected the diverse origins of the artists whose native lands had come under Tamerlane's rule. The inscriptions on the brass ewer include two odes of Hafiz, a fourteenth-century poet of Shiraz in Persia.

There was also much drinking. Drunkenness and overeating were an esteemed part of Mongol tradition, and there was almost a ritual quality to Chagatai drinking bouts. Clavijo, a teetotaler, noted sourly that "the man who drinks very freely and can swallow the most wine is called a hero." Ibn-Arabshah, also disapproving, reported that at this time, Tamerlane "ate and drank things forbidden" to a good Muslim and quickly became as drunk as his warriors. "And he remained in this condition amid zithers, harps, lyres, organs, and pipes; amid dancers, singers, and things wonderful and rare. And the Tempter urged him until pleasure and bounding joy made him light and agile, and he linked his arm with another's and stretched out his hand to one who rose before him, and they helped each other with arms joined. And when he was in the midst of dancing, he tottered amongst them, because of his lameness."

Infirm and aged though he now was, Tamerlane was not to be prevented from embarking on the planned invasion of China, and in October 1405, the expedition set out from Samarkand. The weather was bitter and the army suffered greatly. Its weary generals enforced a halt at Otrar, on the Syr Darya River and still within Tamerlane's domains, and another three-day drinking bout ensued. Together with the bleak climate, this excessive overindulgence took an inevitable toll on the ailing Tamerlane, and he fell sick. Eating nothing but still drinking quantities of arrack, a coarse alcoholic spirit, he started to vomit blood. At last, in the words of ibn-Arabshah, "the butler of death came to him with a bitter cup." He died at Otrar on February 18, 1405.

Up to his final sickness, Tamerlane had been hardy and physically resilient throughout his life. Ibn-Arabshah described him as a tall, large-headed man with a beard, thickset and very strong. (This impression was confirmed when Tamerlane's grave in Samarkand was opened by the Soviet Archaeological Commission in 1941; they found, according to Professor Gerasimov, "the skeleton of a man, who though lame in both right limbs, must have been of powerful physique, tall, and of a haughty bearing.") Powerful, energetic, and courageous, Tamerlane was above all a warrior: This was both his strength and, when he is compared to the other great empire builders of his time, his weakness.

Tamerlane's empire was to prove less durable than that founded by his predecessor Genghis Khan. Divided among his generally unimpressive descendants, the empire fell apart in the course of the early fifteenth century, while those of his great ene-mies—the Ottomans and the Mamluks—revived. Tamerlane had never sought to establish a large and sophisticated civilian administration of the kind possessed by his rivals, and consequently the empire lacked a resource that might have provided stability and continuity after the great warlord's death. Nor were there any generals of genius capable of maintaining the momentum of conquest. Tamerlane himself was the single great leader of the Chagatai army; he had no true heirs, and without the sense of purpose and direction that he had provided, the army had no reason to exist.

Tamerlane was the last of the great nomad conquerors to menace the settled civilizations of the Near East, India, and Europe. In the course of the next few centuries, the introduction of firearms would shift the balance of military power in favor of infantries and the gunpowder empires of the West. While Tamerlane lived, Samarkand had claims to be the center of the known world. In the centuries that followed, earthquake, fire, and neglect would lay waste to those architectural foundations that were the most pleasing of Tamerlane's achievements, and Samarkand itself would return to the relative obscurity from which he had briefly raised it.

GREEN AND TRANQUIL PLACES

The restorative and consolatory pleasures of gardens have rarely been as prized as in the troubled fourteenth century. Taking inspiration from the East, where gardens had for centuries provided the ideal setting for rest, music, intellectual discussion, or the pursuits of love, Western rulers and their subjects sought refuge from warfare and natural calamities within shaded and flowery enclosures.

Soon after his return from the Crusades in Palestine in 1274, Edward I of England established a garden at the Palace of Westminster that included fruit trees, willows, lilies, and peonies, as well as several hundred red and white roses. Edward's first queen, Eleanor of Castile, brought gardeners from Aragon in Spain to work on her estates. The royal gardens confirmed the increasing influence of the Islamic tradition of garden design, which was already well established in Sicily, Spain, and Italy.

Since the fall of the western Roman Empire in the fifth century, northern gardens had been mainly utilitarian, intended for the propagation of fruits, vegetables, and medicinal plants and herbs. But now, benefiting from a range of plants—wallflowers, stocks, hollyhocks—introduced from the East, gardens became places for enjoyment and leisure as well as for work. The illustration on the right, from a fourteenth-century Italian manuscript of a medical treatise, emphasizes the beauty of the setting rather than the health-giving properties of the plants.

In the arid lands of Persia and the Middle East, gardens had been perceived since the rise of Islam in the seventh century as mirrors of the paradisiacal garden of sensuous delights to which the faithful would be admitted after death. The earthly appeal of gardens was no less important: Protected by high walls from the encroaching sands, flowers and fruit trees offered the only available color and shade. Around his capital of Samarkand, the fourteenth-century Mongol conqueror Tamerlane laid out at least fifteen gardens with orchards, lakes, palaces, and pavilions.

Farther east, the most influential gardeners were the Chinese and Japanese, whose gardens were designed as microcosms of the rich variety of the universe, intended to appeal to the intellect as well as to the senses. Forsaking symmetry, the gardens of the Orient imitated more closely than Islamic or Western gardens the contours of the natural landscape, but the arrangement of rocks, streams, and plants had a precise symbolic significance.

Riding out of the barren desert, a Persian prince seeks entry to the lush garden that surrounds the castle of his beloved.

Water—for desert dwellers, the most precious of the elements—was the lifeblood of all Islamic gardens. In the private retreats of rulers, enclosed within the palace precincts, water sprayed from fountains and mirrored the sky from tiled pools; in extensive parks, often built outside city walls, it ran in streams or more formal conduits, cooling the air and pleasing the ear as well as irrigating the plants.

Both types of garden are depicted in the fourteenth-century Persian miniatures shown here, which illustrate scenes in the courtship of a legendary Persian prince and a Chinese princess; the background of fertile abundance suggested the sensual and the spiritual pleasures of love.

Seated on a dais above a lawn studded with hollyhocks, irises, and daylilies, the prince and his consort are served sweets. A wineskin cools beside the stream in the foreground, while behind the lovers, attendants gather roses.

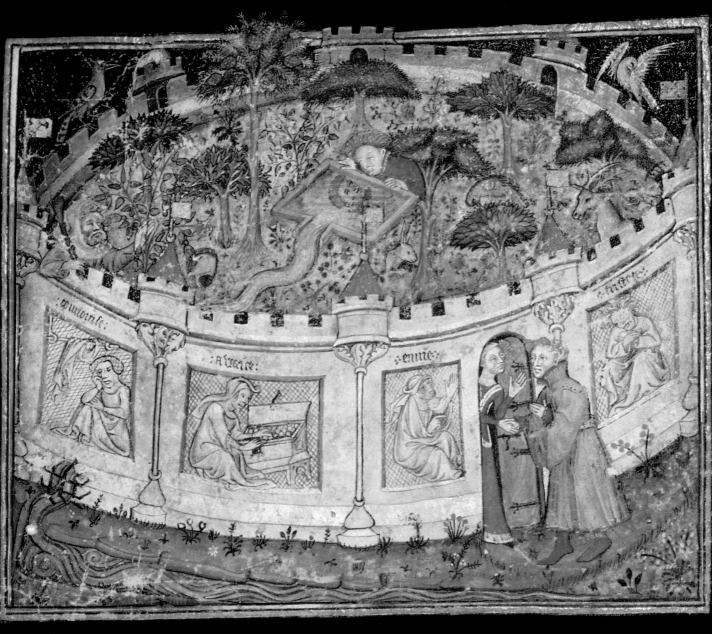

A miniature from a manuscript of the *Roman de la Rose* shows a supplicant at the gate of the Garden of Love. Within, a still pool reflects the visage of Narcissus, a legendary Greek youth of great beauty; even birds and animals are protected from harm.

EUROPE: HAVENS OF DELIGHT

During the fourteenth century, the aesthetic influence of Islamic gardens was carried from southern into northern Europe, where kings, courtiers, and churchmen took pleasure in small, intimate sanctuaries surrounded by walls or trees. Pathways were shaded by grapevines on rows of wooden arches; flower seeds broadcast over the grass turned a plain lawn into a "flowery mead." Gardens in literature assumed a symbolic importance as refuges from worldly ills: The setting of the first part of the *Roman de la Rose,* a thirteenth-century French allegorical romance, is the garden of the god of love, and the storytellers in Boccaccio's *Decameron* flee from the Black Death ravaging the cities to the verdant estates of country villas.

CHINA: NATURAL HARMONIES

Originating several centuries before the birth of Christ, the Chinese tradition of garden design reflects ancient beliefs about man's place in nature. The apparent randomness of winding waterways, rocky hills, and bamboo pavilions—in contrast to the formal symmetry of Chinese domestic architecture—was guided by principles of harmony and composed of balances between rough and smooth, vertical and horizontal, male and female forms. Gardens were also arranged as a series of views, like scenes in a scroll painting. In the fourteenth century, they were widely cultivated by highborn scholars denied public office under the Yuan dynasty of the Mongols.

Flowers favored by the Chinese included gardenias (above), chrysanthemums, peonies, and lilies. The gardenia's white petals were used to decorate women's hair and to perfume cosmetics and tea.

In one of two pavilions in this fourteenth-century painting, a scholar entertains a monk. The second pavilion is surmounted by a towering rock; such formations were valued as natural sculptures.

JAPAN: IDEAL LANDSCAPES

Japanese gardens were strongly influenced by Chinese models, but by the fourteenth century, several native traditions had developed. Smooth, flat-topped stones, as introduced by the Zen priest Muso-Soseki in his temple garden in Kyoto in 1339, came to be preferred to the rugged shapes favored by the Chinese. Gardens were often laid out to evoke archetypal landscapes: Small hills and mounds suggested a mountain scene; ponds and stones represented a lake or sea studded with islands. The aim was to capture the spirit rather than to represent literally the particular features of the chosen landscape, an emphasis also apparent in the importance accorded to pruning, where the goal was to coax from each plant its essential form.

The twisting trunk of a
pine tree, symbol of lon
gevity and forbearance
under stress, and an up
right flowering tree rise
above rocks and a swirling
stream in a noble's garden

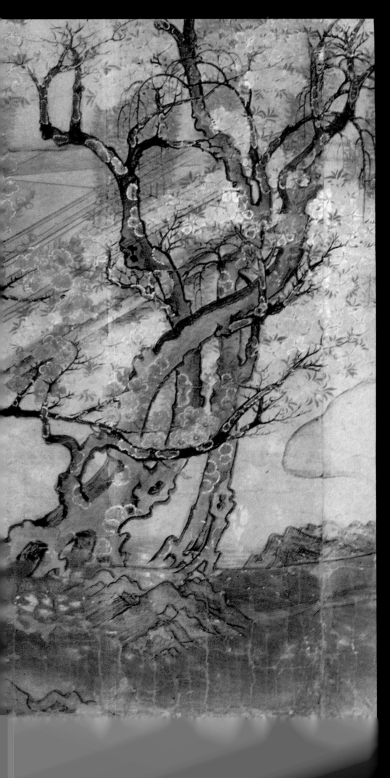

A fourteenth-century scroll
shows a scholar enjoying
the blossom of a cherry or
plum tree *(far left)* and
peach trees from an open
terrace. The cherry was
the most prized of the
flowering trees, and enthu-
siasts sat up on spring
nights waiting for the first
blooms to open at dawn

CHINA'S BRILLIANT DYNASTY

"Build up the walls high; store grain bountifully; proclaim yourself emperor slowly." This was the advice given by an aged Chinese scholar to a young rebel leader named Zhu Yuanzhang in 1358. The implied message was that power would naturally accrue if Zhu kept his defenses and his supplies well tended, and the emphasis on security and food was understandable at the time. Floods, famine, and drought in the first quarter of the century alone had claimed more than seven million lives, and when these recurrent natural disasters abated, the Chinese people were no less at risk from roaming bands of brigands and the corrupt local administration of the occupying Mongols who ruled their country. For the peasants especially, basic survival was the only realistic goal.

As the son of destitute tenant farmers, Zhu Yuanzhang had experienced the sufferings of the people firsthand. His parents and brothers had all starved to death while Zhu was in his teens, and Zhu himself had survived only by entering a Buddhist monastery as a novice. He was courageous, ruthless, and intelligent but could hardly have believed when he first joined a band of rebels in 1352 that he would eventually rid China of its foreign rulers and, as emperor himself, found the illustrious Ming dynasty, which would rule the nation for almost 300 years.

For a man of humble birth, such a destiny was made possible only by the conditions of anarchy and political chaos that had overtaken the Yuan dynasty of the Mongols. The Yuan rulers were descendants of the tribal warriors of the central Asian plateau who, under Genghis Khan a century earlier, had acquired by terror and conquest the largest empire the world had known. By Chinese standards, the Mongols were barbarians. But their rule, at least in its early years, was not totally injurious, and by conquering the northern as well as the southern domains of China, they had reunified a divided empire.

The north of China, ruled in the twelfth century by the Manchurian Chin dynasty, had been overrun quite rapidly. Its arid plains, windswept and bitterly cold in winter, were excellent terrain for the Mongol cavalry. The populous and fertile lands that surrounded the Yellow River had proved alarmingly exposed, and the Mongol horsemen reached the valley of the Huai River, marking the frontier between the two halves of the nation, by 1234.

Southern China, the seat of the native Song emperors, was more difficult to conquer. The climate was warmer and far wetter; there were great lakes and innumerable canals. Substantial barriers against invasion, mountain ranges cut off the tropical southern coast from the Yangtze valley, blocked the way to Burma, and surrounded the fertile basin of Sichuan on the upper Yangtze. In this lusher terrain, the Mongols had to master the techniques of fighting among canals and rice fields. When Kublai Khan—the grandson of Genghis—came to power in 1260, he built fleets of ships to

The pockmarked skin, bulbous nose, and protruding jaw of Zhu Yuanzhang, the peasant rebel leader who rose to become the founder of the Ming dynasty, are vividly rendered in this anonymous caricature; but also apparent are his fierce intelligence and strength of character. Ruthless, he ousted the Mongols, China's previous rulers, and destroyed his real or suspected opponents; firm and decisive, he brought stability to China after decades of civil war. When Zhu proclaimed the new imperial dynasty in 1368, he followed Chinese tradition in choosing a title for his reign, which also became his title; he was known from then on as the Hongwu emperor, or emperor of "Boundless Martial Valor."

carry his armies across the Yangtze and the great lakes and along the coast. Aided by the technical skills of many of his new Chinese subjects—and also by dissension among the enemy generals—Kublai made steady progress; and in 1271, he proclaimed that the mandate of heaven had passed to his new dynasty, for which he took the name Yuan ("Origin"). The last native armies held out in the deep south for seven more years; rebellions occurred at intervals for far longer; but by the latter decades of the thirteenth century, all of China was firmly a province of the Mongol Empire.

The Yuan capital was in the north, well beyond the Yellow River and almost on the edge of the arid plains, at Dadu (now Beijing). For the Mongols, this city provided easy access to their other steppe kingdoms, which extended westward to Persia and the borders of Catholic Europe. There Kublai built his palaces and pleasure gardens; there he commanded his great hunts, riding in a gilded tower carried by four elephants; and there the wealth of northern and southern China was brought as tribute.

Most of the Mongol troops who had fought for Kublai settled in the north, around Dadu. Strong Mongol detachments were also located along the Grand Canal, which since the seventh century had linked the lower reaches of the Yangtze and Yellow rivers and was essential for transporting grain supplies from the fertile south to the northern capital as well as around Nanjing in the lower Yangtze rice bowl. But apart from these troops, neither the garrisons nor the civilian officials who controlled Yuan China were from the conquering race.

Lacking administrative skills themselves, the Mongols organized Chinese society in such a way as to exploit the talents of their subject peoples. Yuan law recognized four categories of citizens. Very much in the first place were the Mongols themselves, who were encouraged to remain a military aristocracy. Next came other aliens known as the *semuren,* the "people with colored eyes." For the most part, these were Muslim subjects of Mongol-controlled empires beyond the great deserts; they included Persians, Arabs, Turks, even the occasional European. Their reliability was ensured by the fact that, as foreigners in China, they were wholly dependent on Mongol power; the Yuan used them to control the financial administration. Almost as dependable, and far more numerous, were the *hanren,* or "people of the north": the Chinese inhabitants of the northern provinces and their non-Mongol neighbors, Khitan, Jurchen, Koreans, and so forth. Last and most numerous were the *nanren,* the southerners of the conquered Song empire.

The Mongols' knowledge of the country they ruled remained slight, since in routine matters they depended on reports made by the semuren, who themselves often relied on Chinese clerks and interpreters. But China under their rule was not at first illgoverned. Trade and agriculture began to flourish again after the disruption caused by the invasions; canals and waterways were restored and extended; the civilian bureaucracy was permitted to carry out its work without military intervention. And the native Chinese, whose northern provinces especially had been frequently overrun by nomadic barbarians, had long experience of alien cultures and had developed their own ways of coming to terms with foreign rule.

In the past, the Chinese had assimilated and ultimately absorbed their conquerors by converting them to their own traditional principles of government. Derived from the teachings of Confucius, a Chinese philosopher of the sixth century BC, these precepts provided the ethical and political framework for an ordered, hierarchical society in which the general welfare of the people was the central concern of thoughtful and enlightened rulers. The dissemination of Confucian ideas was the responsibility of highly educated scholars who believed that long and thorough study of the Confucian classics and of history would produce a truly civilized person uniquely qualified to hold public office. In practice, the scholars came from a restricted number of families, well under five percent of the population; but even such a minority, in populous China, amounted to multitudes. Before the Mongol conquest of China, the better scholars had been selected from the many aspirants by three competitive public exams, on which recruitment to the civil service depended.

The victorious Mongols at first had no time for Confucian learning. They tolerated Confucianism as they tolerated most of the other beliefs among their diverse subjects: Buddhism; animism; the ancient Chinese blend of philosophy and magic known as

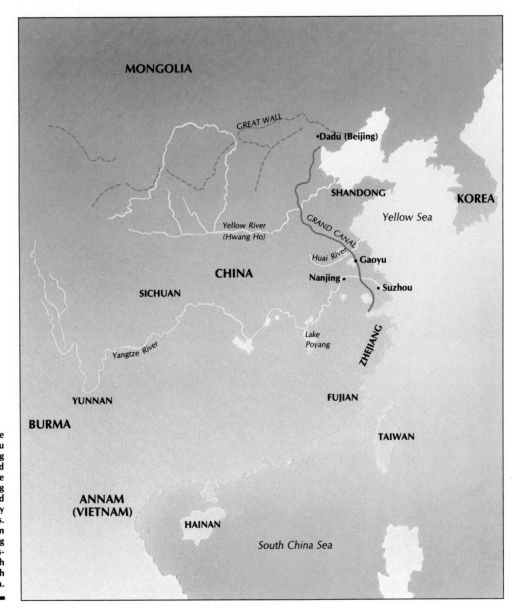

In the early fourteenth century, China was ruled by the Yuan dynasty of the Mongols from their capital at Dadu in the north, close to their original homeland. Following successive floods and famines, rebellions occurred throughout the central and southern provinces. The rebel leader Zhu Yuanzhang seized the city of Nanjing in 1355; after defeating rival leaders at Suzhou and farther up the Yangtze, he confirmed his supremacy by ridding northern China of the remaining Mongol forces. By the time of his death in 1398, Yunnan had been incorporated into the empire and the rule of the Ming was firmly established. The Ming capital was transferred from Nanjing to Beijing in 1420; in the sixteenth century, Ming emperors built the Great Wall, which extended some 1,500 miles inland from the Yellow Sea.

THE WAY OF THE SCHOLAR

Under the Mongol Yuan dynasty, native-born Chinese were barred from high office, and the educated classes, who for centuries had provided the nation with its chief bureaucrats, were deprived of their livelihood. Some highborn scholars continued to serve the government in a lowly capacity, but many more adopted reclusive lives in which they devoted their talents to literature or painting. Among the latter was Ni Zan, an artist and poet who, along with other masters of the fourteenth century, developed a style of landscape painting remarkable for its purity and delicacy.

Born into a wealthy landowning family, Ni Zan sold or gave away almost all his possessions during the 1350s to avoid the heavy taxes levied by the Mongols, and thereafter he lived as a wanderer on his houseboat. Most of his paintings depicted trees, rocks, and a horizon of distant mountains across an expanse of water; devoid of people, their austerity expressed his detachment from the turmoil of rebellion.

Ni Zan, the subject of this fourteenth-century portrait, prepares to compose a poem. A servant offers water, which will be mixed with ink in the inkstone on the painter's right. On the screen behind Ni Zan is a landscape typical of his spare and disciplined work.

Daoism; Islam; and the various brands of mostly heretical Christianity—notably Nestorianism, whose doctrines derived from a Syrian theologian of the fifth century—that had penetrated central Asia. But in the generations after the conquest, the Mongols and their allies who were brought up in China came to respect Confucian teachings; had all gone smoothly, the Yuan dynasty might have been thoroughly absorbed into the ancient modes of Chinese government.

Yuan politics, however, were distinctly turbulent. The Mongol throne was always held by descendants of Genghis Khan, but the succession was determined by the methods traditional among the warring tribes of the steppes, which often involved armed force and fratricide. The thirty-nine years after Kublai's death in 1294 saw ten emperors ascend and descend the throne, often very suddenly. Partly, the quarrels among the Mongols were tribal or personal; partly, they reflected a political argument as to whether the Yuan rulers should retain their Mongol identity or whether they should adjust and conform to the native traditions of China.

In 1315, the emperor Ayurbarwada reintroduced examinations based on Confucian texts to recruit officials for the civil service. The Mongols and their allies were allowed to take different examinations from the Chinese and were admitted into the service at higher grades, but to the Chinese scholars who had continued to teach in Confucian academies, the omens seemed propitious. They were given further encouragement when Togh Temur, the nephew of Ayurbarwada, came to the throne in 1329. A poet and calligrapher with a fine appreciation of Chinese culture, Togh Temur ruled through Mongol and semuren generals whose power was concentrated in the Chinese heartlands, and thus China became increasingly detached from the Mongol-controlled empires to the west.

If Togh Temur had lived a normal span, the Mongol dynasty might have become fully assimilated. But he died at the age of twenty-eight, in 1332; and after the customary tumult, the throne passed to his young nephew Toghon Temur. Real power, however, lay with the grand chancellor, Bayan, a Mongol of great ability and with a fierce determination to follow the old ways. In 1335, Bayan abolished the civil-service examinations; he reserved all the higher administrative positions for Mongols and semuren; and he made laws prohibiting the Chinese from learning the Mongol languages or bearing arms.

Bayan had his reasons. Floods, famines, and epidemics, many of them caused by a series of abnormally cold winters, had left much of China enfeebled, and there were frequent rebellions in the southern provinces. Mongol control had been weakened by power struggles among claimants to the imperial throne. The entry into the civil service of examination graduates—in Bayan's eyes, smooth-talking Chinese with no practical experience—had spread discontent. Bayan had a radical economic program to restore prosperity—he aimed to encourage agriculture, close down superfluous government workshops, reduce spending on construction, and cut taxes—and he wanted people he could trust in vital positions.

But such peremptory measures aroused fierce opposition. In 1337, popular rebellions broke out across central and southern China, only to be suppressed with considerable bloodshed by Bayan's troops. Strange rumors then began to circulate about the chancellor's next intentions: He would ban not only weapons but iron tools; he would seize all unmarried boys and girls for government service; most horrifying, he intended to kill all Chinese who bore the names of Zhao, Zhang, Li, Liu, or Wang. This was a large section of the population, and although the ghost of

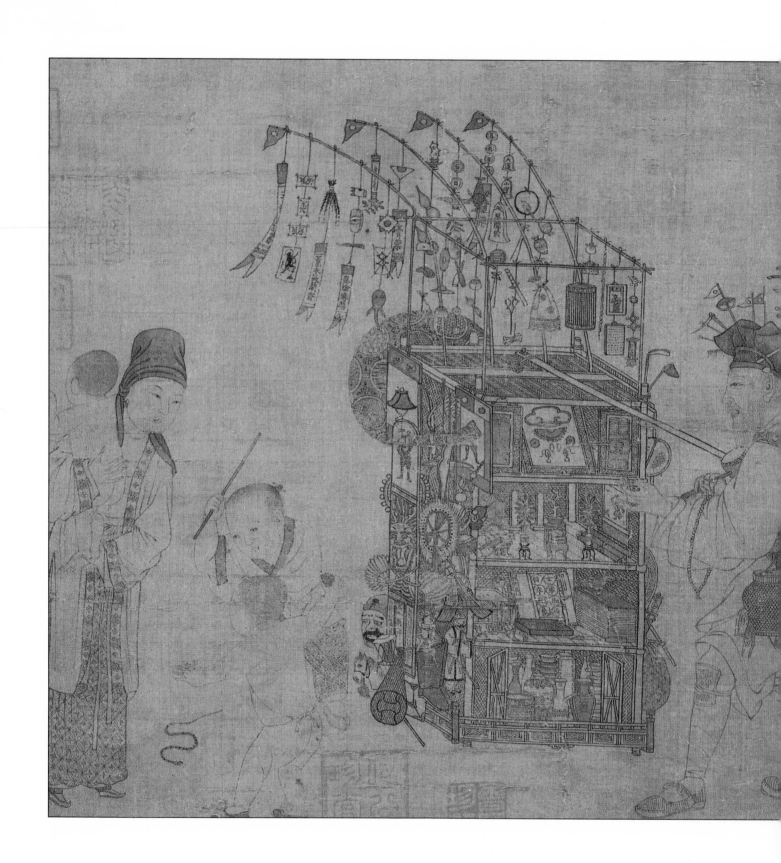

Genghis Khan might have approved of such a remedy, it is doubtful whether Bayan really had such plans. In any case, his quarrel with the Chinese left him dangerously exposed in Mongol politics, as did his engrossment of all the great offices of state, which brought him temporary security and enormous wealth but left every other contender unsatisfied. In 1340, Bayan was overthrown in a coup led by his own nephew, Toghto. He died on his way into exile.

Toghto sincerely admired Chinese ways. He restored the examinations, cancelled Bayan's persecutions, commissioned a history of the Song dynasty, and in 1344—in a sublimely Confucian gesture—resigned the chancellorship to give his rivals an opportunity to deal with the political problems he confronted. He was eventually replaced by Berke Buqa, a Mongol who was learned in Chinese literature and who intended to govern China by classical precepts. But this triumph of official Confucianism had come too late, for by now Mongol political and military control of China had become dangerously precarious.

Bayan's suppression of the rebellions of 1337 was to be the last great assertion of Mongol power. With no serious foreign enemies, many of the Mongols who held hereditary military office had become indolent and incompetent. The common soldiers were exploited by their commanders; their training was neglected, and some were forced to work at civilian trades, either to replace their military pay after it had been embezzled by the administration or to raise an income for their generals. Some had never learned how to use their weapons. In many garrisons, most of the troops had vanished, leaving their commanders to pocket their pay.

Apart from the imperial guards stationed around the capital, the government could by now command few reliable forces. Bandits infested not only the mountains but increasingly the productive plains. And the local levels of Yuan civil government, beneath the authority but not under the control of Mongols and semuren, had long been distressingly corrupt.

The central government was aware that all was not well. Civil-service examination questions in the 1340s indicated a determination to select candidates with a realistic grasp of the problems: "Some say that if the regulations are strict and salaries adequate, clerks will not become corrupt. But nowadays the regulations are strict and salaries adequate, yet clerks are still corrupt. How do you explain this?" Unfortunately, Confucian principles of government, however well intentioned, were no longer an adequate remedy for the troubles afflicting China.

Among the lower classes of native Chinese, the teachings of Confucius were vaguely respected but hardly understood. More deeply rooted were various brands of popular religion, which had traditionally provided channels for the expression of discontent. The ancient popular dream of returning to a more primitive society free of state interference had always been fostered by Daoism, for example, and Daoists had formed secret societies that encouraged rebellion against the government. Under the Yuan dynasty, this subversive role was taken over by the Buddhists, with steadily increasing popular support.

The teachings of Buddha had been considerably reinterpreted since their introduction into China in the second century BC. The passive, passionless life preached

Painted in ink on silk at the beginning of the fourteenth century, a street peddler hawks bric-a-brac while two young children strike at a toy snake on the ground. Itinerant merchants selling food, medicines, household goods, and children's playthings were a commonplace sight in all Chinese towns, where traditional patterns of daily life continued uninterrupted during the years of Mongol occupation.

by the Indian sages was no longer the ideal. By the fourteenth century, the most popular Chinese version of Buddhism declared that worshipers should hope not for peace in the next world but for salvation in this; and that Maitreya, the Buddha of the Future, would descend to earth and establish the Pure Land in which Buddhists would rule. These doctrines were spread by the White Lotus society, a secret organization that, as discontent under Yuan rule intensified, began to preach that the coming of Maitreya was imminent.

Blended with Buddhism in the teachings of the White Lotus was another creed from outside China—Manicheanism, the Persian religion that sees all things as a conflict between the forces of light and of darkness. Chinese Manicheanism taught that in the final conflict, the Prince of Light, Ming Wang, would appear to redeem the world. In the popular mind, this figure was not entirely distinct from the Buddhist Maitreya.

At some time during the 1330s, the clandestine religious fraternities became openly political. Unlike the Confucian elite, who were prepared, even anxious, to assist the new dynasty, many of the common Chinese had never seen the Mongols as anything more than foreign barbarians who stank of mutton. The Chinese themselves were pork eaters, and they possessed a far more sophisticated culinary tradition than the nomadic Mongols. The White Lotus now taught that the Mongols were nothing less than the primeval forces of darkness and that the Pure Land could be achieved by restoring the Song dynasty of southern China.

Tradition accords the leading roles in the White Lotus rebellion to a Buddhist monk, Peng Yingyu, and to one Han Shantong, who proclaimed himself the rightful heir of the Song empire. Their disciples met at night in secret; they swore blood brotherhood, took ritual names, and planned to raise an army whose troops would be distinguished by the wearing of red turbans. To the Chinese, this was a symbol of great significance: It recalled two Daoist secret societies that had rebelled against past usurpers, the Red Eyebrows and the Yellow Turbans. In addition, red was the traditional color of the legitimate dynasty.

In the 1340s, a network of Red Turban conspirators developed in the valleys of the Yangtze and the Huai rivers. They were aided by the vagaries of a third waterway, the Yellow River, which in 1344 burst its banks and began to change course, veering north and flooding vast areas. In these floods, the Grand Canal, which ran northward from the Yangtze by way of the Huai, was overwhelmed, silted up, and blocked.

The only route for transporting essential grain supplies to the north was now by sea, around the Shandong peninsula. This voyage had always been perilous and was made more so from 1348 by the activities of one Fang Guozhen. By his own account, this southern Chinese trader in the highly taxed commodity of salt had been falsely accused of piracy and was forced to murder a prominent official. Thereafter he took to piracy in earnest and found the grain convoys an easy target. Unable to suppress him, the Yuan court sought Fang's goodwill by offering him an official title.

In this critical situation, Toghto returned to office as grand chancellor in 1349. He decided to reopen the Grand Canal and to redirect the Yellow River into its original southern course. He acted with determination, enterprise, and administrative skill, but by assembling 150,000 laborers in the Huai valley to clear the vital canal, he played straight into the hands of his enemies.

Floods, famines, brigands, and turmoil had caused great hardship in the valley, and the White Lotus society had its strongest support among the peasants of this region. The conscripted laborers were equally discontented. Tradition holds that the White

This clay model of a farmstead, interred in the tomb of a Ming landowner, demonstrates a ground plan typical of all Chinese buildings from the emperor's palaces downward. The living quarters were arranged on a north-south axis, with the main family rooms around an inner courtyard and those of the servants and guests around an outer enclosure. The blank north wall—to the rear of the main two-story dwelling—and the screen behind the entrance in the south wall were intended to prevent the invasion of evil spirits. Most buildings were constructed of brick or clay between load-bearing timbers; the slopes of their tiled roofs were elegantly curved, and sculptures of animal spirits—believed to protect against fire—crowned their ridges.

Reception hall

Family dwelling

Outer courtyard

Inner courtyard

Screen

Entrance pavilion

Lotus spread a rumor that the end of the evil empire would be announced by the appearance of a one-eyed giant and arranged for a one-eyed statue to be buried where the laborers would uncover it.

The conspiracy erupted into rebellion when Toghto, aware that trouble was brewing, ordered the arrest and execution of Han Shantong, the Song pretender. Far from disabling the Red Turban forces, this produced a wave of furious rioting. The pretender's son Han Liner escaped from custody, and the summer of 1351 saw the collapse of Mongol authority everywhere in the Huai valley and along the Yangtze. Hordes of central Asian tribesmen sent to restore the situation were routed by the Red Turbans. The Grand Canal, which Toghto's efforts had largely repaired, was blockaded by rebels led by an enterprising salt smuggler named Zhang Shicheng, who declared himself emperor.

Still, the Yuan dynasty commanded considerable loyalty in regions where the Red Turban conspiracy had not penetrated. Although the Red Turbans counted many prosperous Chinese among their ranks, they were essentially a revolutionary movement and as such were automatically opposed by Chinese landowners. And Toghto responded heroically to the crisis. Accepting that the north would have to feed itself, he organized an emergency program of state-sponsored agriculture that brought nearly 154,500 square miles north of the Yellow River under cultivation; he printed enormous amounts of paper money to boost government revenue without raising

This fifteenth-century painting depicts an informal meeting of officials held in the garden of Yang Rong *(seated, third from right)*, a senior officer in the Ming administration. While servants attend to food and drink, a court painter in the center of the picture records the occasion on a scroll laid out on a table. All these officials had gained their positions by succeeding in the civil-service exams reintroduced by the Hongwu emperor after the Mongol occupation; the emperor also prescribed the scarlet robes of office worn here by Yang Rong and one of his colleagues. The robes of civil administrators were embellished with auspicious birds, such as the white crane and the golden pheasant; military officers sported wild beasts, from lions for the most senior generals to sea horses for the most junior.

taxes; and by 1354, his loyalist armies had won a string of victories. The only serious resistance came from Fang Guozhen the pirate, inaccessible in his island lairs off the southeastern coast, and from Zhang Shicheng the smuggler, who had shut himself into the city of Gaoyu, which blocked the Grand Canal.

During the winter of 1354, the Yuan forces, led by Toghto in person, closed in on Gaoyu. The last of Zhang's armies was defeated; the city was besieged; final victory was in sight. Then a letter arrived from the capital: Toghto was dismissed from his post. His success had aroused envy at court; not satisfied with taking away his position, his enemies had him sent into exile and poisoned. His army subsequently disintegrated, and many of his soldiers joined the rebel forces. Zhang was safe, at least for the moment.

Rebellion now spread rapidly throughout China, and by the end of 1356, the Yuan emperor controlled only the area around his capital of Dadu. Elsewhere in northern China, power lay with Mongol or Chinese generals who were nominally loyal to the Yuan, but who in practice were concerned largely with their own safety. The southern coast was mostly dominated by Chinese leaders loyal to the Yuan, but the pirate Fang Guozhen ruled the coast of Zhejiang south of the Yangtze, and between the loyalist areas, the surviving Red Turbans still controlled the rich Yangtze valley and the Huai. The followers of Han Liner, the "Young Shining Prince" and self-styled Song emperor, held the northern parts of the rebel territory and battled with the forces loyal

to the Yuan emperor; in the southern parts, in the Yangtze valley itself, four rival centers of power emerged.

The smallest but best organized of these power bases was ruled from Nanjing by Zhu Yuanzhang. Born in 1328 about 100 miles northwest of the city, Zhu was a tall and spectacularly ugly peasant whose beady eyes, pockmarked skin, bulbous nose, and jutting chin made him an obvious butt for jokes on his own name, which sounded the same as the word for "pig" in Chinese. In 1352, he had enlisted in the forces raised by a fortuneteller who believed in the imminent descent of the Maitreya Buddha; he had then recruited his own band of followers, starting with twenty-four childhood friends from his native village, and won a series of victories against Mongol and other Chinese troops. In 1355, he had crossed the Yangtze River with 30,000 men and seized Nanjing. Zhu remained, in name at least, a vassal of the restored empire of the Song pretender.

Around the mouth of the Yangtze, the richest of the rebel domains belonged to Zhang Shicheng, who had moved south after his miraculous delivery at Gaoyu and captured the wealthy city of Suzhou in the same week that Zhu took Nanjing. There, as ruler of 10 million subjects, he lived in a luxury he could not have dreamed of when he had rowed illicit cargoes through the marshlands.

Upstream from Nanjing, in the lands around the central Yangtze, the Red Turban uprising had never accepted the Song pretender's leadership. The rebel armies there were led by a fisherman named Chen Youliang, who awarded himself the title of Emperor of Han, recalling an even earlier dynasty. Needing boats to ferry his army over the wetlands of the Yangtze and the great lakes that it feeds, Chen had formed an alliance with the leader of an inland pirate fleet who armed himself like a Japanese samurai and was therefore known as Two-Swords Zhao.

Above the gorges that led to Sichuan, the fourth of the rebel domains in the south was ruled by an isolated army of Manichean rebels.

Except in the north, where the Mongols defeated the Song pretender and forced him to flee south, this patchwork rebellion spent most of its energies in internal disputes. Of the three rival leaders along the Yangtze—Zhang at Suzhou, Zhu at Nanjing, and Chen upstream—the strongest appeared to be Zhang, who had come to terms with the Yuan and arranged to supply Dadu with grain to be transported by the fleet of the pirate Fang. But each was strong enough to repel the Yuan forces or any one rival. All three progressed rapidly from bandit leaders to rulers of organized states, and they modified their zeal for apocalyptic revolution accordingly.

In 1359, Chen Youliang, the "Emperor of Han," determined to break the deadlock by seizing Nanjing in a sudden, waterborne attack. For this he needed Two-Swords Zhao's ships; but he did not entirely trust Zhao, whom he therefore summoned to a conference and beheaded. The fleet was incorporated into the main Han forces, which in 1360 sailed downriver. After landing outside Nanjing, however, they fell into an ambush; Zhao's former followers deserted wholesale, and Chen was lucky to escape with half his troops.

The next year, Zhu counterattacked. He now had sufficient ships to sail up the Yangtze and invade the Han empire. The rival fleets met in a fierce naval battle on Lake Poyang; the Han had the worst of the encounter, losing more than 100 ships, but Chen withdrew upstream with his survivors, and Zhu was prevented from advancing farther by rebellions among his conquered cities. When Zhu returned in triumph to Nanjing, a gust of wind blew a banner around him as he was about to enter

A section of China's Great Wall, punctuated at roughly 500-foot intervals by watchtowers, follows the twisting contours of a mountain's flank in northeastern China. The high stone wall was built in the sixteenth century to replace an earlier line of forts and earth ramparts. It served as a barrier against Mongol princes who, long after the Hongwu emperor had driven the Mongols out of China, lurked threateningly across the northern border. In addition to its military purpose, the wall fulfilled the administrative function of separating the settled Chinese population—who could be taxed and conscripted—from their nomadic neighbors.

the city; he took this as an ill omen and entered by another gate, thus escaping a band of assassins who had been waiting to kill him. Zhu's senior general, the author of this plot, was executed and his place taken by Xu Da, one of Zhu's childhood friends.

In 1363, while Zhu's forces were engaged on their eastern front against the troops of Zhang Shicheng, Chen Youliang planned a second attempt to seize Nanjing. He assembled a mighty fleet of three-decker galleys; each vessel was painted vivid scarlet, had turrets for archers armored with iron plate, and could carry more than 2,000 soldiers. Chen's armada came down the Yangtze on the spring floods; the western cities of Zhu's territories were besieged.

Against the advice of his generals, Zhu gathered all the troops who could be spared from the eastern front—the chronicles say about 200,000—and sailed upstream to attack Chen. Once again the fleets met on Lake Poyang, in a battle that lasted for four days. Zhu was forced to execute several of his commanders before the others would agree to attack the monstrous, seemingly invincible scarlet galleys of the Han fleet. After the initial encounter with the Han, however, the smaller Nanjing vessels escaped to the shallower parts of the lake, from where they attacked using fireships loaded with gunpowder and manned by crews willing to sacrifice their lives. Directed into the tightly packed ranks of the enemy galleys, these fireships caused a blaze in which more than 60,000 Han soldiers perished. Zhu's ships then withdrew by night to the mouth of the lake adjoining the Yangtze; when the surviving Han galleys attempted to break out, they were ambushed and routed. Chen himself was struck dead by an arrow in the eye.

Zhu's victory established him as the strongest of the Red Turban leaders, and in 1364, he proclaimed himself Prince of Wu—the traditional name for the lower Yangtze region. From leader of a band of rebels Zhu had become the undisputed ruler of a kingdom, and the imperial throne itself was now a realistic goal. The remains of the Han empire were incorporated into Zhu's domains; then, reinforced, he turned on Zhang Shicheng in Suzhou. After ten months of siege, Suzhou surrendered to Zhu's general, Xu Da, in 1367; Zhang hanged himself in the ruins of his palace, and Zhu was left supreme in southern China. Earlier that year, the Song pretender had drowned—or had been drowned—while crossing the Yangtze.

In January 1368, the new imperial dynasty was proclaimed at Nanjing. Except for the Yuan, former dynasties of China had taken their names from the estates of their founders, but such a title was not available to the successful bandit Zhu Yuanzhang. He chose instead the epithet of Ming, or "Brilliant"; this had unmistakable echoes of Ming Wang, the Shining Prince whom the Red Turbans awaited to redeem the world. The new emperor decreed that his reign should be known by the title of Hongwu, or "Boundless Martial Valour." (After his death, he was known as Taizu, or "Great Progenitor.") He declared that Nanjing would be the new imperial capital; and from that southern city he set out to conquer the north.

Never before had the north of China been conquered from the south; all previous conquests had been of the south by the north. But the Hongwu emperor's position was so strong that he was able to overcome both the north and the deep south in the same year of 1368. By attacking the Yuan, the Ming ruler claimed the loyalty of all true Chinese. "As for our Chinese people," announced the emperor, "it must be Heaven's will that we Chinese should pacify them. How could the barbarians rule them? I fear that the heartland has long been stained with the stink of mutton, and the

This lacquer panel from a chest of drawers made for a Ming emperor depicts legendary creatures traditionally associated with the ruling dynasty. In Chinese myth, dragons were not ravaging monsters but beneficent water spirits that controlled the clouds and rain; the five-clawed dragon at right, which was portrayed only on imperial property, symbolized the emperor's power and his care for his people. The plumed bird at left represented the empress; it appeared only in times of prosperity and was thought to be responsible for the warmth of the sun and the abundance of the harvest.

people troubled. Therefore I have led forth the armies to make a clean sweep. My aim is to chase out the Mongol slaves, to do away with anarchy and assure the people of their safety—to cleanse China of shame."

Xu Da, with a quarter of a million men, marched north for an effectual cleansing. The Yuan government in Dadu had little power to fight back. Deprived of revenues, it printed paper money by the cartload; but the troops this should have paid also existed only on paper. Local leaders fought fiercely but with no coordination. The last Yuan emperor, immured in his palace, devoted himself to the esoteric rituals—sacrifices of human hearts and livers and Tantrika ceremonies indistinguishable from common orgies—that were taught by the Tibetan Buddhist monks he favored. As Xu Da's multitudes approached, the emperor fled from Dadu back to Mongolia. Only the Mongol warlord Koko Temur offered stern resistance; he held onto the northeastern provinces and for some years maintained a war on the Ming frontiers.

The conquest of the deep south proved even easier. The pirate admiral Fang Guozheng had made offers of collaboration to the future Ming emperor as early as 1359; now, submitting to Hongwu's imperial power, he offered him ships to transport the Ming army along the coast. The Yuan warlords in the south mostly surrendered on good terms, with one prominent exception. Chen Youding was an illiterate peasant who had been a policeman before the Red Turban uprisings; in suppressing the rebels, he had shown great courage and martial skill, and as provincial governor and commander of an army loyal to the Yuan in the southern province of Fujian, he held out against the invaders until forced to surrender in February 1368. Captured by the Ming army and brought to Nanjing, he was offered a pardon but replied: "The state is demolished, my family is gone. I shall die. What more is there to talk about?" He was put to death, but a shrine was built in his memory, for the emperor admired courage and loyalty even in his enemies.

After 1368, the Ming armies fought only on the frontiers. Mongolia was invaded in 1370; Toghon Temur, the last Yuan emperor, died, and Koko Temur fled into the central Asian desert. The Red Turban state of Sichuan was suppressed in 1371; the defenders had slung chains across the Yangtze gorges from which they hung platforms with stone-throwing catapults, but the advancing Ming fleet smashed these with cannon fire. In 1372, Xu Da led an army across the Gobi Desert as far as Genghis Khan's old capital of Karakorum, but he suffered heavy casualties at the hands of Koko Temur's surviving forces, and the Ming armies did not invade Mongolia again for thirty years. In 1382, they made one final conquest, of the Mongol princedom of Yunnan in the far southwest.

Sky   Water   Earth

The ingenuity of Chinese artisans was nowhere more apparent than in the transformation of the liquid resin secreted by the lacquer tree into a medium for decoration. The technique of building up many layers of lacquer in which a design could be carved was widely practiced under the Yuan dynasty and reached its peak in the imperial workshops of the Ming emperors.

Over a wood base, a smooth foundation was prepared by applying layers of lacquer mixed with fine clay or ash; these were followed by coats of lacquer mixed with a pigment, which was traditionally red or black. In all, as many as 200 coats of lacquer were required to provide a surface that was deep enough to be carved; each coat—only a fraction of a millimeter thick—took at least three days to dry and was rubbed down with fine pumice to remove any flaws. The carved decoration extended over every part of the lacquer surface; expanses of earth, water, and sky were represented by stylized patterns of squares, diamonds, or interwoven lines that formed starlike shapes.

In factories that were supervised by a member of the imperial household, different artisans specialized in painting on the lacquer, polishing it, and carving the design. These artists supplied not only the court but also private collectors with a range of products that included trays, bowls, and containers for incense, sweetmeats, or cosmetics such as the early-fifteenth-century box shown at left.

Having conquered an empire, the Hongwu emperor now set about ruling it. Concerned to establish the legitimacy of the dynasty he had founded, he performed the traditional ceremony of plowing a furrow of soil at the altar dedicated to Xian Nong, a legendary emperor of antiquity. He regularly performed the religious rites required of the emperor, sacrificing to earth and heaven after the manner of the ancient dynasties; he fasted and prayed for rain at the appropriate seasons; and as a means of ensuring protection, he granted official court titles to the guardian spirits of all the city walls of China. Nor were the walls themselves neglected. Nanjing was rebuilt as the new capital, with a separate imperial precinct enclosing the palaces and temples that were the heart of the Ming realm. The walls of the new capital stood almost sixty feet high and nearly nineteen miles long.

Bolder measures than these, however, were required to restore stability and prosperity. The great rebellion, as well as decades of natural disasters such as floods and famine, had caused much loss of life, and China's population in the 1370s was at least one-third less than it had been in the previous century. The Hongwu emperor forcibly resettled great numbers of families in the northern provinces, where the effects of Mongol rule had produced utter devastation. He imposed heavy taxes on the former domain of his rival Chen around Suzhou, which he suspected of disloyalty. He initiated ambitious irrigation and drainage works that did much to restore the economy, and there was a massive investment in woodlands—more than one billion trees were planted for their fruit and timber.

Confucianism flourished at the new court, although in his heart the emperor always favored the Buddhist teachings of the monastery in which he had served before joining the rebels. Now that he was in power, however, he disassociated himself from the ideas of the Red Turban revolutionaries: He protested that he had never supported their messianic dreams, that he had been compelled to join their forces for reasons of self-preservation, and that the great rebellion had been an appalling and unnecessary catastrophe. At the same time, he maintained that his rise to power through that rebellion was a clear indication of heaven's desire.

The Hongwu emperor's attitude toward his imperial predecessors was equally ambiguous. He offered sacrifices to the spirit of Kublai Khan, but at the same time he banned the use of Mongol names and dress and declared his intention to restore the Chinese civilization that the Mongols had destroyed. He had a clear perception of why the Mongols had failed: The court had lost control over the lower levels of government, which—as he knew from personal experience—had become incompetent and avaricious, destroying the weak and forcing the strong to resort to banditry. This was not to be allowed, but to prevent it, the emperor relied considerably on methods of violent compulsion that hardly differed from those tactics employed by the Mongols before him.

Some of his reforms in government, nevertheless, were constructive and innovative. He set up a nationwide tax system directly responsible to the central administration to replace the corrupt semuren tax collectors employed by the Mongols. He ordered an accurate land survey and census to achieve justice in taxation, and he imposed great order on civil society. All of China was divided into "communities" of 110 neighboring families, of whom the 10 most prosperous took turns to provide a headman to represent the community in its dealings with government officials. The other 100 families were divided into groups of 10, who took turns providing communal labor services. Each community had to provide a school, an altar, and a

THE FLOWERING OF MING PORCELAIN

The world-renowned blue-and-white porcelain that was produced in great quantities under the Ming was in fact first made under the Tang dynasty, which ruled China from the seventh to the tenth centuries. During the fourteenth century, trade among the Mongol-controlled countries of Asia stimulated foreign demand for the products of Chinese kilns. The import of cobalt—from which the distinctive blue color was derived—from Persia was interrupted during the years of rebellion, when copper red was used in its place. But after the Ming became established, production of blue-and-white porcelain in the imperial workshops was stepped up.

The decorative designs were painted on a hard paste of powdered china stone mixed with kaolin, or white china clay, which was then glazed and fired. The quality of the porcelain depended on the availability of raw materials; the best kilns were at Jingdezhen, near Lake Poyang, which was surrounded by rich china-clay deposits.

A floral pattern decorates this late-fourteenth-century ewer. The copper-red coloration that was used for this and similar Ming vessels generally resulted in less crisp designs than those achieved with cobalt blue.

Phoenixes, dragons, clouds, and flowers swirl over this porcelain vase—one of a pair that was presented to a Buddhist monastery in 1351.

The shape of this early-fifteenth-century vase, known as a "precious moon flask," derives from Syrian glassware, but the naturalistic, uncluttered design is purely Chinese.

charitable granary, and each was required to hold monthly meetings at which their problems could be discussed.

This very regimented society was administered by a civil service that was in many ways thoroughly traditional. The uniforms of the court and provincial officials were modeled on those of the Tang dynasty, whose rule over a unified empire in the seventh and eighth centuries AD was remembered as a golden age. The structure of Chinese government, with its intricate bureaucracy that advised and might even censure the emperor, had been preserved intact even under the Mongols, and under the Hongwu emperor, the same conventions were at first observed. The examination system aroused his suspicions—he had a peasant's prejudices against book learning—and most of his high officials were appointed through personal recommendation. In 1370, however, he instituted new examinations that included tests in archery and horsemanship as well as the Confucian classics. Candidates were selected from a nationwide system of state-supported Confucian schools that, as the emperor had intended, recruited talent from a wider section of Chinese society than ever before.

But the background and personal history of the founder of the Ming were in striking contrast to those of the highborn rulers of previous native dynasties, and this difference was manifest in his attitude toward authority. To the Hongwu emperor, as to the Mongols, government meant obedience to orders from above. He continued the Yuan practice whereby even the highest officials lay prostrate throughout any imperial interview, and he ruled with a severity perhaps inevitable in one who had ruthlessly survived desperate crises. The Yuan had fallen through lax administration; those who disobeyed the Ming ruler could expect no mercy.

The emperor understood full well that ferocious punishment is a crude and often ineffectual instrument of justice. He was struck by the comment of the ancient sage Lao Tzu that those who do not fear death cannot be deterred by the death penalty, and in some cases, he substituted forced labor for summary execution. "When a young man does wrong and is executed," he wrote, "he leaves behind his parents, a young wife, and a young son. And if you think about it, they will be in need of food and clothing; they will feel sorrowful and full of memories, sighing ceaselessly night and day. Gods and men, too, grieve to hear about this sort of thing."

But however horrified the Hongwu emperor claimed to be at the suffering he felt bound to inflict, he could not trust his subjects to be virtuous simply by their own inclination. He rigorously suppressed all secret political or religious organizations; and for as long as the slightest danger of insurrection remained, he felt unable to relax his vigilance. If his own most powerful general could betray him—as at Nanjing in 1362—who was to be trusted? A successful rebel can never feel wholly secure, and the Hongwu emperor had deep-seated reasons for insecurity. He could not forget the time when "I lived in a village with only my shadow for company, and who listened to my orders then?"

In 1380, the emperor's suspicions brought about a crisis that was to overshadow not just the rest of his reign but those of his heirs also. The empire had encountered problems: permanent, unwinnable wars against tribesmen on the frontiers; the despoiling of the coast by Japanese buccaneers; the determination of Chinese merchants to maintain contact with foreigners, in defiance of the emperor's wishes. The Hongwu emperor came to believe that all these problems were due to his chancellor, Hu Weiyong, an old comrade who had served him since 1355. Hu had appointed many senior civil-service officials, and as part of his duties, he had dealings with

Shown at ease in their garden on a fifteenth-century silk scroll, two scholars handle ancient bronze and ceramic objects with appropriate reverence. After the turmoil of the Mongol occupation of China, many educated Chinese took a renewed interest in their native cultural heritage, and artists looked to the past for models of excellence. The bronze phoenix bearing a wine cup at right, decorated with inlaid gold and silver, was made around the fourteenth century in the style of the Zhou dynasty, which had ruled China 2,000 years before.

powers beyond the frontiers. The emperor became convinced that his chancellor had used his position to foster a monstrous conspiracy aimed at overthrowing the dynasty with armed support from abroad. Whether or not the plot in fact existed, Hu perished; and after his execution, an ever-expanding network of accusations and forced confessions brought death to more than 30,000 officials because of their supposed association with the disgraced chancellor.

After 1380, the Hongwu emperor trusted nobody. He abolished the office of chancellor and with it the secretariat, the department through which the chancellor had coordinated the lesser ministries. He also did away with the office of chief military commander. Thenceforth the Ming emperor held all central power himself.

In the long term, this was the most important of the emperor's decisions. His distrust of senior officials became institutionalized; never again would the power of a Chinese emperor be balanced or restrained by the advice of a trained civil service, as had been usual under the Tang and the Song dynasties. Given a strong and resolute ruler, such as the Hongwu emperor himself, the autocracy functioned; but under more incompetent or indolent rulers in later generations, this system was a recipe for disorder.

The immediate effect of the emperor's paranoia was to bring disaster to millions of innocent Chinese. The surveillance officers whose work was to find treason duly reported it, whether it existed or not; one fortunate survivor of their investigations remarked that the sinless Buddha himself would have been lucky to escape accusation. The destruction of Hu Weiyong's associates was followed by further purges in which ministers, generals, and even the emperor's own nephew perished. For minor errors, court officials were flogged, an indignity unthinkable under previous dynasties. Poets were executed for writing of natural calamities, which were seen by the emperor as allusions to his own harsh rule. Ministers made final farewells to their wives and families before setting out to report to the palace and rejoiced if they returned alive.

In this climate of fear and suspicion, corruption flourished. Here, too, the emperor was merciless, but his efforts met with only limited success. One particular granary clerk accused of embezzlement, a certain Kang Mingyuan, was twice branded, then hamstrung, and then lost both kneecaps, but still he continued to pilfer government supplies. The emperor was baffled; he wrote that he "hoped to control villains on the idea that if one man is punished, a hundred will take warning. But people's minds nowadays aren't like this." When even officials of the Board of Punishments were found guilty of corruption, the Emperor "gave them countless lashes, I cut off their feet, and I showed all this to the other members of the Board. With my own eyes I witnessed this punishment and my hair stood on end because of it. I was sure that there would be no repetition of the crime. But while the survivors were still in terrible

GUARDIANS OF THE AFTERLIFE

The rulers of the Ming dynasty, with the exception of the Hongwu emperor, were buried outside Beijing, which became the capital of their empire in 1420. The highway that was built as an approach to their tombs was known as the Spirit Road *(opposite);* it had a gentle curve to frustrate evil spirits, which were believed to travel only in straight lines, and the road was guarded by colossal sculptures of humans and beasts, each one carved from a single block of stone.

The twenty-four animals—twelve standing and twelve lying down—included camels, elephants, and mythical creatures; it was said that the beasts changed position at midnight, so that those who had stood during the day could take their turn to rest at night. The twelve standing male figures comprised soldiers, civil servants, and imperial counselors to serve the spirits of the deceased emperors in the afterlife.

One of their number was the monumental warrior shown clad in armor at left; wearing the uniform of a senior Ming general, he holds in his right hand a commander's mace, while his left hand clutches his sword hilt. Resembling in their impassive majesty archaic statues from the Song and Tang dynasties, this warrior and his companions linked the Ming dynasty with an earlier era regarded as a golden age of Chinese civilization.

pain and bleeding, and the corpses of the others had not yet been taken away, more misconduct occurred. I don't know how the world can be securely ordered."

One way of ordering the empire was to entrust it to his own family. The Hongwu emperor had twenty-six sons, and he gave hereditary principalities to all of them. But he was unwilling to grant them any real independence and retained personal control of their garrison armies. In 1395, he issued a decree that deprived the princes of many privileges, including the right to appoint their own staffs.

In his last years, the Hongwu emperor attempted to reform his obstinate people by having the young learn by heart his proclamations, and in 1397, nearly 200,000 pupils gathered in Nanjing for a competition in reciting the Emperor's Great Announcements. But the benefit of all such measures was uncertain, and in 1398, the Hongwu emperor died disillusioned. "Despite my exhaustive efforts, I can't transform bad people, whether they are clever or stupid. I always think things through completely before imposing them on my subjects, yet after a long time nothing produces any results. Alas, how hard it is!"

The emperor's pessimism was not without cause, but his words of self-criticism do not do full justice to his achievement. He had ruled over the greatest empire on earth, and he left it unified and at peace within its borders. The thirty years after his death were a period of dynamic activity in which, building upon the stable political structure established by Hongwu, his successors consolidated the strength of the new dynasty at home and abroad. The Grand Canal was dredged and repaired, and the capital of the empire was moved to the old Mongol site of Dadu, which was renamed Beijing. Ming armies subjugated Annam (present-day Vietnam) and defeated a new threat from the Mongols in the north; naval expeditions exacted tribute from territories as distant as Zanzibar. China, under native rulers, had regained its greatness.

Midway through the fifteenth century, the emperor was captured by the Mongols. Thereafter, although the dynasty itself survived and the empire remained intact, the spirit of adventure and inquiry that had characterized the early decades of the Ming declined. Under a series of less able rulers, seaborne trade was banned, the army retreated behind the defenses of the Great Wall—stretching across the empire from the Yellow Sea to central Asia—and Ming China reverted to its founder's policy of isolation from the outside world. As a result, little significant scientific or technological progress was made during the following two centuries of Ming rule. But for the vast multitudes of Chinese peasants—whose sufferings the Hongwu emperor had known firsthand—this loss of dynamism was an acceptable price to pay for the return of stability after the turbulence of Mongol rule and the decades of internecine strife between rival rebel armies.

MARTIAL PASTIMES

During the fourteenth century, when few regions in Europe or Asia remained untroubled by invasion, rebellion, or civil war, sports and leisure in every class of society took on an increasingly martial aspect. As well as reflecting the violent tenor of the age, this trend followed gradual changes in the ways that armies were organized and battles conducted.

Seeking skilled bowmen in 1337, just before the outbreak of war with France, Edward III of England prohibited all sports except archery on pain of death. On every village green, young men became proficient in the use of the longbow *(right)*, and standards of archery soared. Warfare in Europe had for centuries been perceived in terms of the valorous deeds of highborn knights, and Edward's action was tacit recognition of the growing discrepancy between this chivalric ideal and the reality of combat. His initiative bore fruit on the battlefields of Crécy and Poitiers, where the destruction of the proud knights of France by the English longbowmen proved that well-trained archers were no less valuable than cavalry.

In countries outside Europe as well, there was a new emphasis on training and discipline. The armies of Islamic countries had traditionally been made up of professional warriors, whose ranks included many slaves, supplemented by urban militias and tribal auxiliaries drawn from the nomadic peoples within the state's control. During the fourteenth century, from Egypt and the rising Ottoman Empire eastward, the importance of the professional soldiers increased while that of the other groups declined. Training became standardized, and manuals concerning horsemanship, weaponry, and tactics were compiled.

The links between military and peacetime pursuits were perhaps stongest among the tribal societies of central Asia, which were permanently geared for warfare. Wrestling was the traditional sport of the Mongols, for example, and young boys—and often women—had been trained for centuries in the skills of archery from horseback, which were vital in hunting as well as in war. Recognizing the value of these skills and of their continual practice, the Mongol conqueror Tamerlane made organized hunts a regular part of the training of his mounted warriors.

EXERCISING THE MIND AND BODY

Aside from weaponry, the most important factors in warfare were good generalship and brute strength. In many countries in the Middle Ages, the intellectual and physical aspects of military training were fostered respectively by the game of chess and the sport of wrestling.

Probably attaining its modern form in India in the sixth century, chess was closely associated with military strategy, especially in Persia. The many military commanders who took a keen interest in chess included Tamerlane, who is said to have named one of his sons after the piece known as the rook, which he happened to be moving on the chessboard at the time he was informed of that son's birth.

Wrestling, the oldest of warrior sports, was by the fourteenth century practiced in a number of different styles governed by national conventions. In Persia, Mongol-style wrestling was patronized by the Il-khan dynasty of the thirteenth and early-fourteenth centuries. In Japan during the same period, sumo wrestling was exclusively promoted among the military caste of the samurai, and public matches were banned. The sport was also an integral part of the training of the knights of the Holy Roman Empire.

A fourteenth-century Persian manuscript miniature *(above)* shows a game of chess in progress between a Persian prince and an Indian envoy. At right, a Spaniard confronts a Muslim opponent in a late-thirteenth-century Spanish illustration. Chess was introduced into Europe around the eleventh or twelfth century, but its relevance to military training remained strongest in the Middle East.

Informal and ritual styles of wrestling are depicted in three fourteenth- and early-fifteenth-century illustrations. English children *(left)* attempt to unseat each other from their bearers; Persian champions *(right)*, dressed in Turkish-style tight-fitting leather pants, display their skills at a prince's court; and Japanese sumo wrestlers *(below)* grapple in fierce combat, the aim of which is to topple one's opponent or force him out of a designated circle.

ACQUIRING EQUESTRIAN SKILLS

Cavalry provided the main strike force of all fourteenth-century armies, and riding skills were held in high esteem throughout the world. European armies relied heavily on the devastating impact of armored knights on their massive chargers; man and beast fought as a single unit, and if the knight was unfortunate enough to be un-horsed, the encumbrance of his equipment made him easy to capture. In contrast, the tactics of the armies of the Middle East and especially of central Asia, where the horses were smaller, sturdier, and swifter, were determined primarily by the speed and mo-bility of their cavalry.

In times of peace, hunting on horse-back—with spear, sword, bow and arrows, or birds of prey—provided ideal practice in horsemanship. Throughout the countries of Asia, such sport was enjoyed by all ranks of society; in European countries, however, where horses were less common and a knight was customarily expected to main-tain a team of two or more mounts, it was almost exclusively a pursuit of the aristo-cratic classes. The richly decorated saddles and harnesses with which wealthy knights furnished their mounts testified to the hors-es' importance both as status symbols and as accessories of war.

Opposing teams of polo players are shown in action in this fourteenth-century Persian miniature. Polo probably originated in Persia, where it provided ideal training for the light-cavalry warfare of the Middle East.

Painted in Chinese style by a Persian or Turkish Muslim artist, a horseman bears a bird of prey aloft on his gloved hand. Hawking from horseback was a favorite pastime of warrior elites in all Islamic lands.

In a miniature from a French treatise on hunting written in the fourteenth century, a noble is shown in pursuit of a wolf that has threatened the flocks of his peasants. As well as providing sport, hunting served to suppress wild animals and to supply game for the table.

In scenes from fourteenth-century manuscripts, an English archer strings a longbow *(left)* by bracing it against his foot, and a crossbowman *(far left)* takes aim at a bird. To preserve the tension in the wood, the longbow was kept unstrung when not in use. The string of the crossbow was drawn back to a retaining catch with an iron hook, seen here in the crossbowman's belt.

A late-thirteenth-century Japanese scroll painting depicts mounted warriors at target practice. Japanese bows, made partly of bamboo and about seven feet long, were so designed that the arrows were loosed "off-center" from a point in the lower half of the bow. Accuracy demanded great skill and years of practice; unlike the English longbow, however, these bows could be used from horseback.

The principal long-distance weapons in the Middle Ages were bows and arrows. In Europe, where the bow was an infantry rather than a cavalry weapon, there was an aristocratic prejudice against archery, but elsewhere this sport was widely practiced by both the nobility and those of lesser rank.

One of the simplest types of bow was the English longbow, which was made from a single piece of wood about the span of a man's height and had a range of almost 1,000 feet; variations of the longbow were used throughout Europe, as well as in Africa and India. More complex was the Asiatic composite bow made of laminated wood, sinew, and horn or bone; short enough to be used from horseback, this was one of the main cavalry weapons of the armies of the Ottomans and Tamerlane.

The steel crossbows widely used in continental Europe had a greater range than the standard wooden bow, but their shooting rate was slower due to the more awkward method of drawing the bowstring. In several Islamic countries during the fourteenth century, the ordinary bow was turned into a form of crossbow by turning it on its side and shooting short arrows along a grooved piece of wood held against the apex of the curve.

A wild deer wounded by arrows flees from a Persian prince in these silhouetted details from a fourteenth-century manuscript. Seated on a high saddle, the prince is using a short, composite bow of the type first developed in central Asia, where it was employed to deadly effect by the Mongols.

A miniature from a fourteenth-century Egyptian cavalry training manual shows a Mamluk rider charging a target. He grips his lance in the two-handed manner common to the Middle East.

Depicted in an Arabic treatise on horsemanship, a mounted soldier holds up his shield while launching his spear. Following convention, the artist has drawn the spear behind the soldier's head rather than across his face.

One of the earliest and simplest of weapons, the spear was used in medieval warfare by both cavalry and infantry in many forms, ranging from the heavy twenty-foot-long pike used by European foot soldiers to the light javelins hurled by Mongol horsemen. Each weapon required specific skills to master its handling, and different exercises were devised to test a soldier's strength, balance, and accuracy.

At the most basic level, these exercises could be played as games by children with pointed sticks. But at their most elaborate, they demanded all the accouterments of war, and the occasions of their practice became popular spectacles.

In European countries, tournaments might often last as long as a week; they included feasting, pageantry, and a variety of mock combats, the most spectacular of which was jousting between mounted knights armed with lances and decked out in elaborate armor.

In Egypt and other Islamic countries, where more emphasis was placed on teamwork and coordination than on individual valor, enormous stadiums were constructed, in which massed squadrons of horsemen performed disciplined cavalry maneuvers in front of crowds of spectators.

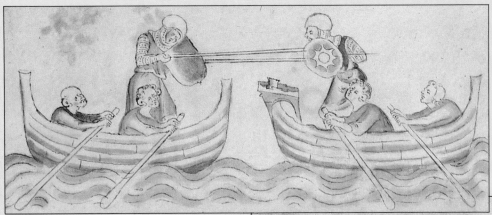

Jousting from boats, competitors armed with lances attempt to hurl each other into the water while maintaining their own balance. This sport, here shown in a miniature from a fourteenth-century English manuscript, was especially popular in Venice.

This fourteenth-century illustration shows a youth tilting at a quintain, or swiveling target. On his follow-through, the boy had to avoid being hit by the weighted sandbag.

To a fanfare, armored knights charge each other in a joust. The triple-pointed lances were used only in tournaments, where the aim was to unhorse an opponent rather than inflict injury. The heavy helmets shown in this fourteenth-century illustration were by then redundant in warfare.

THE AFRICAN EMPIRES

Crowned with a royal diadem, a sturdy bronze statuette of a ruler of the Yoruba kingdom of Ife, in present-day Nigeria, holds in its hands the symbols of absolute power: a beaded scepter and a ram's horn containing magical substances. The sophisticated city-states of Ife and neighboring Benin developed from the eleventh century onward in the thickly forested country south of the sub-Saharan savanna belt; during the fourteenth and fifteenth centuries, these city-states and other West African states shared a wave of commercial prosperity stimulated by trading contacts with the Arab world north of the Sahara.

In July 1324, a seemingly endless caravan of camels laden with gold and precious objects appeared out of the blowing sands of the Sahara in northern Egypt. Winding its way down the scarp from the high desert to the wide floor of the Nile valley, the caravan halted and made camp beneath the looming bulk of the pyramids at Giza, just south of the city of Cairo. The travelers numbered, according to one account, more than 15,000, and they had been journeying for two months across the trackless wastes of the Sahara from the empire of Mali in the region the Arabs called Sudan, or "Land of the Blacks," far to the west of its present-day namesake.

Leading this glittering procession was the emperor of Mali, Mansa Musa, who was making a pilgrimage to Mecca, the holy city of Islam in Arabia. He was not the first *mansa,* or "emperor," to visit Cairo: Some of his predecessors, converted to Islam during the previous century, had traveled through Egypt before him. But in the fourteenth century, Mali had become the most powerful empire in Africa south of the Sahara, and Mansa Musa had deliberately planned his arrival to impress the Egyptians with the wealth of his people.

From their tents, the travelers from Mali could see the domes and minarets that dominated the skyline of the city described by the North African historian ibn-Khaldun as "the metropolis of the universe." At the time, Cairo was one of the largest and richest cities in the world; its population numbered half a million, and its prosperity was based on the trade that passed through its estimated thirty-five markets and 20,000 shops, traveling along age-old routes from India, China, and Indonesia, as well as the African interior, to the cities of Italy, the Byzantine Empire, and northern Europe. Since 1250, it had been the capital of the Mamluk sultanate of Egypt and Syria, and it had developed into a renowned center of learning and of the arts and sciences of Islamic civilization.

The sultan al-Nasir Muhammad wasted no time in dispatching one of his high officials to the pyramids to greet Mansa Musa and place all the resources of state hospitality at his disposal. The official was also commissioned to persuade the royal visitor—with some difficulty, as it turned out—to mix secular activities with his religious enterprise and agree to the meeting with the sultan that protocol demanded. The emissary reported that Mansa Musa was a man of great formality who insisted on communicating only through an interpreter, although it was discovered later that he could speak Arabic.

Three days later, the African king crossed the Nile and was ceremonially conducted into the city of Cairo. Anyone entering the presence of the sultan was required to kiss the ground before him and then to kiss his hand—but for Mansa Musa, a ruler whose own subjects bent low and sprinkled their heads with dust as a sign of reverence when he addressed them, this was a custom difficult to comply with.

Discreetly, a member of Mansa Musa's entourage drew him aside for an inaudible exchange. At last the king declared, "I make obeisance before God who created me," and he bowed to the ground before approaching the sultan.

Everyone breathed again, and the sultan drew his royal guest to his side with brotherly civility. Rich gifts were exchanged between the two rulers; many loads of unworked African gold and other valuables were delivered to the treasuries of Cairo, and in return, the sultan presented Mansa Musa with a palace for his lodging and bestowed upon his party quantities of magnificent robes, caparisoned horses, and precious and beautiful objects, as well as all the provisions they would need for their stay in Cairo and for their journey to Mecca and back.

Between July and October, when the great caravan of pilgrims departed from Cairo, their presence was the sensation of the city. The governor of the Qarafa district of Cairo, where Mansa Musa's palace stood, was especially impressed by the dignity and religious demeanor of the African king and his companions—he said it was as if they stood in God's presence all the time. When Mansa Musa described the traditional practice of his country of giving the most beautiful girls as gifts to the king, he was shocked to learn that this custom had no place in Islam and vowed to repudiate it immediately.

But above all, it was the apparently boundless wealth of the Africans that astounded the Cairenes. The geographer and historian al-Umari, who was employed in the Mamluk administration, reported that Mansa Musa "flooded Cairo with his benefactions" and left no court official without the gift of large quantities of gold. The king's followers swarmed through the markets and bazaars buying everything that caught their eye—silk, clothes, horses and saddles, dancing girls, Turkish and Ethiopian concubines—and at whatever price the seller cared to ask. So much gold was injected into the city's economy by the African visitors that the value of Cairo's currency remained depressed for several years.

From now on, the Arabs of North Africa could no longer regard their distant neighbors as semilegendary beings of strange appearance and even stranger behavior; and during the course of the fourteenth century, the countries of Europe and Asia also began to realize that to the south of the Sahara lay civilizations no less sophisticated than their own. The east coast of the continent was studded with prosperous city-states where traders from across the Indian Ocean flocked to buy goods from the interior; the kingdom of Ethiopia was enjoying a military and religious revival under a new and forceful dynasty; and many inland kingdoms were also flourishing. Their achievements were no less impressive for having gone largely unrecorded.

It was the Sahara itself that had preserved Africa's isolation. Right across the continent from the Atlantic to the Red Sea stretched a band of desert where rainfall was too low and temperature too high for settled occupation. A zone of habitable grasslands and open forest fringed the desert to the south; beyond lay impenetrable rain forests and the great swamps from which the Nile drained northward.

The wastes of the western and central Sahara were traversed for centuries by irregular caravans of merchants, but none of the successive conquerors of the Mediterranean lands of northern Africa—Phoenicians, Greeks, and Romans—were concerned with extending their control beyond the fertile plains of the north. Even the introduction of the camel into Africa from Asia at some time in the first centuries AD did not make the desert a less formidable barrier.

Then, in the eighth century, the culture of northern Africa was decisively changed by the spread of Islam from Arabia. In their language and customs, the Arabs had more in common with the native Berber tribes than any of the previous conquering peoples, and their armies gained control of the north with startling rapidity. The brilliant and coherent civilization established in the wake of this conquest brought a new era of stability and prosperity in which trade thrived and contacts between the Arab world and the peoples of the interior were steadily increased.

The encounter between the Arabs and the sub-Saharan Africans was to have profound and lasting consequences. In the first place, the wealth of the African societies was enormously increased by the trading caravans that regularly crossed the desert; in the second place, the political development of these societies was to be

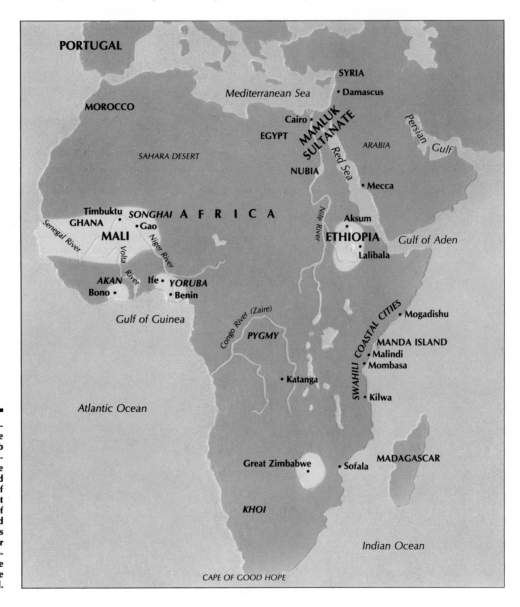

The continent of Africa occupies approximately one-fifth of the globe's land surface; yet until regular trade routes were established across the Sahara after the Arab conquest of the north in the seventh and eighth centuries, most of its population remained isolated from the rest of the world. Commercial contacts eventually led to the rise in the fourteenth century of the empire of Mali in the west and of wealthy city-states along the east coast; at the same time, the inland Christian kingdom of Ethiopia, established in the fourth century AD, enjoyed a renaissance. Most of the central and southern regions were occupied by settled agricultural communities or by seminomadic cattle-raising peoples. The chief exceptions, the Pygmies of the equatorial rain forests and the Khoi of the southern deserts, proved that even in the most inhospitable terrain a livelihood could be forged.

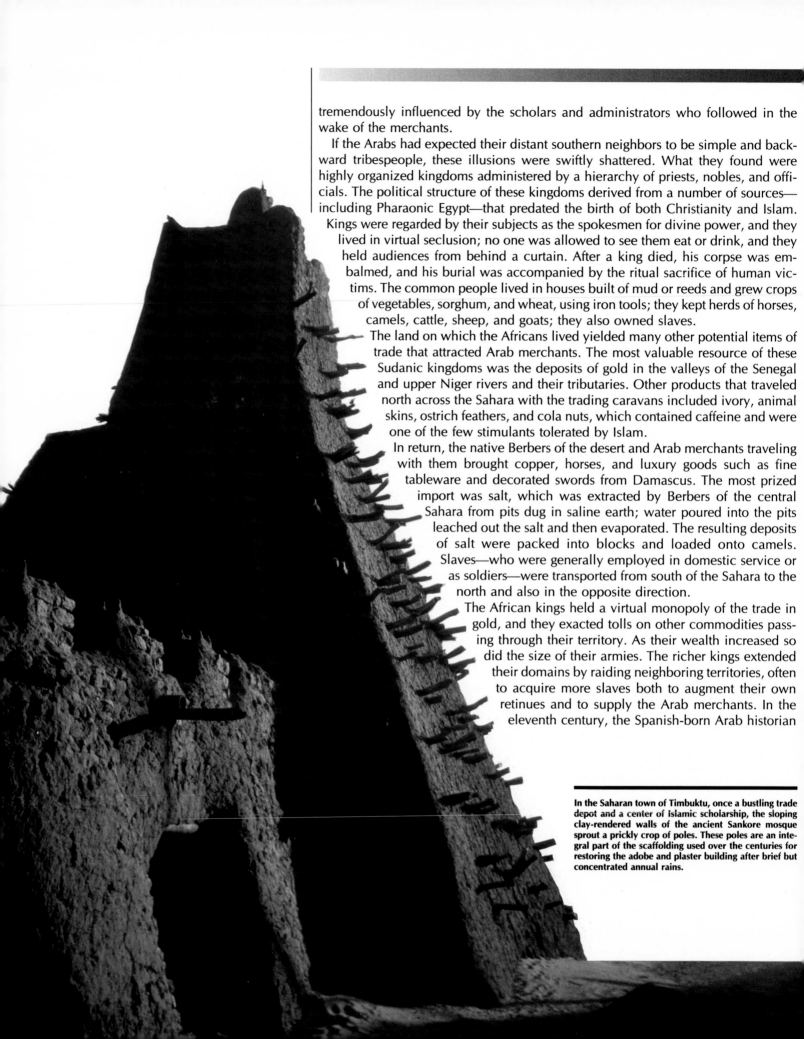

tremendously influenced by the scholars and administrators who followed in the wake of the merchants.

If the Arabs had expected their distant southern neighbors to be simple and backward tribespeople, these illusions were swiftly shattered. What they found were highly organized kingdoms administered by a hierarchy of priests, nobles, and officials. The political structure of these kingdoms derived from a number of sources—including Pharaonic Egypt—that predated the birth of both Christianity and Islam. Kings were regarded by their subjects as the spokesmen for divine power, and they lived in virtual seclusion; no one was allowed to see them eat or drink, and they held audiences from behind a curtain. After a king died, his corpse was embalmed, and his burial was accompanied by the ritual sacrifice of human victims. The common people lived in houses built of mud or reeds and grew crops of vegetables, sorghum, and wheat, using iron tools; they kept herds of horses, camels, cattle, sheep, and goats; they also owned slaves.

The land on which the Africans lived yielded many other potential items of trade that attracted Arab merchants. The most valuable resource of these Sudanic kingdoms was the deposits of gold in the valleys of the Senegal and upper Niger rivers and their tributaries. Other products that traveled north across the Sahara with the trading caravans included ivory, animal skins, ostrich feathers, and cola nuts, which contained caffeine and were one of the few stimulants tolerated by Islam.

In return, the native Berbers of the desert and Arab merchants traveling with them brought copper, horses, and luxury goods such as fine tableware and decorated swords from Damascus. The most prized import was salt, which was extracted by Berbers of the central Sahara from pits dug in saline earth; water poured into the pits leached out the salt and then evaporated. The resulting deposits of salt were packed into blocks and loaded onto camels. Slaves—who were generally employed in domestic service or as soldiers—were transported from south of the Sahara to the north and also in the opposite direction.

The African kings held a virtual monopoly of the trade in gold, and they exacted tolls on other commodities passing through their territory. As their wealth increased so did the size of their armies. The richer kings extended their domains by raiding neighboring territories, often to acquire more slaves both to augment their own retinues and to supply the Arab merchants. In the eleventh century, the Spanish-born Arab historian

In the Saharan town of Timbuktu, once a bustling trade depot and a center of Islamic scholarship, the sloping clay-rendered walls of the ancient Sankore mosque sprout a prickly crop of poles. These poles are an integral part of the scaffolding used over the centuries for restoring the adobe and plaster building after brief but concentrated annual rains.

al-Bakri reported that the king of Ghana—to the north and west of its present-day namesake—commanded an army of 200,000, including more than 40,000 archers. His capital comprised two separate towns—one for the Muslim residents and merchants, one where the king's palace was located—about five miles apart and linked by continuous habitations of stone and acacia wood. The court of the king was in keeping with the wealth of his domain:

He sits in audience or to hear grievances against officials in a domed pavilion around which stand ten horses covered with gold-embroidered materials. Behind the king stand ten pages holding shields and swords decorated with gold, and on his right are the sons of the vassal kings of his country wearing splendid garments and their hair plaited with gold.

Some of the king's ministers were Muslim Arabs whose learning and administrative skills he found useful; and toward the end of the eleventh century, the king, together with many of his nobles and leading merchants, adopted the religion of Islam. This conversion—and also that of other African rulers in the region—was prompted by reasons more material than spiritual. First, it cemented the mutually profitable partnership between the Africans and the Arab traders. Second, although traditional African monarchies had provided effective government for small and relatively isolated states, empires such as Ghana, with one million or more subjects, required new and more complex political systems. Useful models were provided by the administrative, commercial, and legal practices that were integral parts of Islamic culture; and the blending of Arab scholarship with native African customs was to accelerate both the cultural and the political progress of the Sudanic kingdoms.

In 1076, the capital of Ghana was seized by an army of Almoravid Berbers from the western Sahara. Restless raiders rather than organized settlers, the Berbers soon withdrew, but in their wake, the destruction of Ghana was completed by vassal kings fighting to regain their independence and by a neighboring people from Takrur in the north of modern Senegal. In the chaos that ensued, the Malinke people from the small state of Kangaba on the upper Niger were able to assert their own supremacy and found an even more illustrious empire. The Malinke had a strong agricultural base, controlled much of the trade between the grasslands and the coast to the south, and were also fierce warriors. Under their leader Sundiata, a nominal convert to Islam, they defeated the Takrur, who had occupied the old capital of Ghana, at the battle of Kirina in 1240; and by the time Mansa Musa came to the throne in 1312, the new empire of Mali was already the most powerful state in the western Sudan.

Mansa Musa's empire measured more than 1,200 miles from the Atlantic coast in the west to the borders of present-day Nigeria in the east, and about 600 miles from the oases of the Sahara to the rain forests of Guinea in the south. Indirectly, however, Musa's power was even more extensive. Since the middle of the thirteenth century—when the first European gold currency since Roman times had been minted in Florence—the economies of both Europe and North Africa had been based on a common gold standard. The stability of the entire system of intercontinental trade depended on a regular supply of gold—and the most important sources of this supply were the alluvial gold fields that lay within the subjugated territories of Mali. Al-Umari's description of the emperor as "the greatest of the Muslim kings of the Sudan" was not idle flattery: "He rules the most extensive territory, has the most numerous army, is the bravest, the richest, the most fortunate, the most victorious over his enemies, and the best able to distribute benefits."

From interviews with Arabs who lived in Mali, al-Umari obtained detailed information about daily life in the empire. Much of the land was green and fertile, and the hills were covered with trees; crops included rice, sorghum, wheat, and vegetables such as onions, garlic, eggplant, and cabbage. Sheep and goats were not pastured, but they scavenged for food on garbage heaps; gazelles, ostriches, elephants, lions, and panthers roamed freely in the uncultivated regions. The people—"tall, with jet black complexion and crinkly hair"—lived in houses built of pounded clay and roofed with timber or reeds, and wore Arab-style headcloths of white cotton, "which they cultivate and weave in the most excellent fashion."

It was widely reported that the gold of Mali was harvested from the roots of a certain plant that grew on riverbanks and after rainfall in the open country, but one of al-Umari's informants provided a more plausible account: "The gold is extracted by digging pits about a man's height in depth, and the gold is found embedded in the sides of the pits or sometimes at the bottom of them." The hard labor of digging for gold was carried out by pagan peoples who made "much use of magic and poison," and whose kings ruled as vassals of the emperor.

These subject peoples resisted conversion, and even at his court, Mansa Musa was obliged to retain many traditional practices—including that of sprinkling the head with dust as a sign of reverence, and the recitation of odes in honor of the king and his ancestors by court poets—which had no place in Islam. But among the merchants and administrative classes, Islamic customs and traditions were vigorously encouraged. Mansa Musa returned from his pilgrimage to Mecca in 1325 with an Arab scholar and architect in train, who introduced new construction techniques and designs. Mosques and religious colleges for the study of theology and law were built in cities such as Timbuktu, the terminus of one of the main trans-Saharan trade routes. Resident diplomatic missions were maintained in the capitals of Morocco and Egypt, and in Cairo there was also a hostel for students.

Written contracts and the use of credit were now standard practices in commerce and trade. Literacy became important, and although at first it spread only among the important merchants and the bureaucracy of educated officials, it provided a spur to the more general advancement of learning. Timbuktu was destined to become a renowned center of Islamic scholarship in the fifteenth and sixteenth centuries.

Despite the emperor's willingness to make use of the benefits of Arab experience in government, however, Mali retained its essentially African character. Mansa Musa was king, and he allowed no diminution of his absolute authority. Sitting on his ebony throne on a dais encircled by elephant tusks and guarded by warrior slaves, Mansa Musa heard the complaints and appeals of his people and delivered personal judgment. "When one whom the king has charged with a task or assignment returns to him," reported al-Umari, "he questions him in detail about everything that has happened from the moment of his departure until his return."

Mansa Musa died in 1337, but when the Arab traveler ibn-Battuta arrived in Mali fifteen years later, the benefits of his rule were still apparent. Not all of ibn-Battuta's impressions of life in Mali were favorable: "Ten days after our arrival we ate a porridge, which they consider preferable to any other food. The next morning we were all sick." As a devout Muslim, he was shocked by the freedom that he witnessed in relationships between men and women. But for the general conduct of the citizens

A EUROPEAN VIEW OF AFRICA

Southern Africa was unknown territory to fourteenth-century Europe, but some knowledge of the north was gathered from navigators and travelers engaged in commercial trading. A leaf from an atlas produced in Majorca in about 1375 for King Charles V of France shows the most up-to-date information then available. It includes not only the coastlines of southern Spain *(top left)* and northern Africa but also notable landmarks in the African interior with explanatory legends, two of which are translated below.

South of the sloping barrier of rocks that represents the Atlas Mountains is the seated figure of Mansa Musa, ruler of Mali, whose fame had spread throughout Europe. Below the orb in the emperor's outstretched hand is marked the city of Timbuktu; behind him is the town of Gao.

1 "This region is occupied by people who veil their mouths; one sees only their eyes. They live in tents and have caravans of camels. They have beasts from the skins of which they make fine shields."

2 "This black lord is called Musa Mali, king of the black people of Guinea. So abundant is the gold found in his country that he is the richest and most noble king in all the land."

of Mali and their system of government, his praise was unreserved: "One of their good features is their lack of oppression. They are the farthest removed of people from it and their sultan does not permit anyone to practice it. Another is the security embracing the whole country, so that neither traveler there nor dweller has anything to fear from thief or usurper."

Mali was defended by an army in which warriors mounted on Arab horses and armed with lances and bows predominated. Superbly effective in open savanna country, this cavalry was virtually useless in the dense tropical forest that stretched southward between the savanna and the coasts of modern Ghana and the Ivory Coast, and the people in these woodlands never came under the rule of Mali. But these forest peoples, living in small communities around the houses of their kings or in larger walled towns, were not immune to the consequences of what was happening to the north of them. Their territories had for centuries been infiltrated by northern migrants, and the increasing demands of Mali and the other states of the savanna for gold and cola nuts in particular—both for their own use and to supply the Arabs—accelerated this process. Great quantities of gold were dug from shallow mines in the forests or washed from alluvial deposits along the riverbanks. And as with the kingdoms of the Sudan, trade brought new wealth to the peoples who controlled the supply of sought-after commodities.

By the fourteenth century, three major city-states had emerged close to the northern edge of the forest, all ruled by kings believed to be invested with supernatural powers. To the west of the Volta River was Bono, founded by the Akan people; to the east were the Yoruba cities of Ife and Benin. Although Muslim traders from the north were active in all the market settlements of West Africa right down to the coast, the cultural traditions of these states remained largely impervious to Islamic influence. Conspicuous above all were the artistic talents of the Yoruba people, who since the eleventh century had produced life-size sculptures of human heads in bronze and terra cotta that were probably used as effigies in state funerals. These native traditions continued to thrive during the years of trade with the savanna states and long after the arrival of European traders on the southern coast in the sixteenth century, which decisively altered the established patterns of commerce.

Over the course of the fifteenth century, the empire of Mali was to be successfully challenged by the Songhai, a subject people who lived on the eastern borders of the realm around the city of Gao on the Niger River. Although they defeated the armies of Mali in battle, the Songhai were not loath to adopt and further refine many of the administrative practices introduced by Mansa Musa, in the process establishing a form of professional civil service and appointing regional governors for their provinces. The African kingdoms of the Sudan thus followed an unbroken course of expansion and development into the modern age.

While Mali flourished in the west, fortunes were also being made on the opposite side of the continent. And in the east as well, trade—which demanded that produce be effectively marketed and supplies protected—was the spur to new developments among African societies.

The long eastern coast between Mozambique and the Horn of Africa, where Somalia juts out below the mouth of the Red Sea, was where voyagers across the Indian Ocean from India, Indonesia, and even China first disembarked on the African continent. In the ninth century, traders from the east side of the Persian Gulf founded a settlement on Manda Island, near the present-day border between Somalia and

VISAGES OF MAJESTY

No African works of art have greater serenity and dignity than the life-size sculpted heads created by the Yoruba people of Ife, a kingdom in the south of present-day Nigeria that flourished between the eleventh and fifteenth centuries. The terra cotta at right and the copper and bronze heads on the following pages show a sensitive naturalism without parallel elsewhere at the time.

Terra-cotta sculptures of fired, unglazed clay display signs of a continuous evolution from an earlier iron-age culture located in northern Nigeria. The bronzes were produced by an intricate process known as "lost wax," which the Yoruba began to use around the eleventh century. This method involved modeling beeswax over an earthenware core, encasing this in a mold of fine clay, then heating the clay mold to liquefy and remove the wax, and pouring molten metal in its place.

The bronze heads were probably employed in the funerary rituals held for the all-powerful priestly rulers of the kingdom. The funeral ceremonies were held some time after the death of the kings, whose corpses were buried immediately because of the hot climate.

The holes around the statues' hairlines could have been used for fixing real crowns to the heads; similar holes around the necks perhaps enabled the heads to be fastened to wooden effigies. The bronze heads were either held for safekeeping in the Ife royal palace or buried at known spots beneath the trees of a sacred grove, whence they were disinterred for reuse in rituals as the need arose.

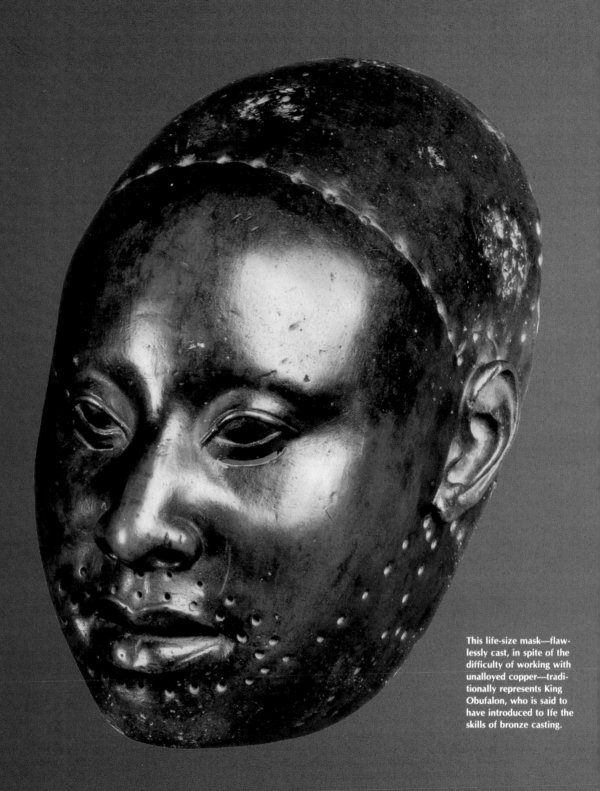

This life-size mask—flawlessly cast, in spite of the difficulty of working with unalloyed copper—traditionally represents King Obufalon, who is said to have introduced to Ife the skills of bronze casting.

The delicate features of this nine-inch-high bronze head may indicate that it portrays a female ruler. The fine vertical lines that emphasize the skillful modeling of the face probably represent a Yoruba scarification pattern.

Kenya; local Africans, who quickly learned about seafaring and the practices of long-distance trade from these and other foreign merchants, founded their own settlements along the coast and in northern Madagascar. But not until the late thirteenth century, following a great wave of Muslim expansion into India and Indonesia as well as eastern Africa, did these settlements come of age as flourishing centers of international trade.

The products of East Africa that attracted foreign merchants were rich and varied. Ivory, tortoiseshell, incense, and spices were staple items of trade, but ships leaving the east-coast ports also carried iron ore from the mines around Malindi and Mombasa, copper and tin from Katanga (in the southwest of modern Zaire), and gold from Zimbabwe in the south. Just as Europe's hunger for gold was fed by Mali, so the mines of East Africa supplied Arabia and India. The principal imported goods were cloth and beads, used for barter and decoration, but luxury items such as Ming porcelain from China and stoneware from Thailand testified to the wealth and sophistication of the merchant communities.

During the fourteenth century, there were more than thirty major ports along the coast, from Mogadishu in the north to Kilwa and Sofala in the south. Their African populations were skilled fishermen and farmers as well as traders, and they spoke a form of Bantu, the most widely dispersed family of languages in Africa. Out of the continuous mingling of these Bantu-speaking Africans with Arab merchants there developed a distinctive, urban-centered culture known as Swahili—in Arabic, "people of the coast." The Africans adopted the Islamic faith and incorporated many Arabic words into their own language, and Swahili became the everyday speech of all the east-coast centers of trade.

The governors of these cities built mosques, palaces, and forts of coral stone. Some were ruled by Arab sultans who ousted the local chieftains. According to an anonymous Swahili historian who wrote a history of Kilwa in the early sixteenth century, the leader of the first Arab traders to reach this settlement had purchased the offshore island from its African ruler. "The newcomer to Kilwa said: I should like to settle on the island: Pray sell it to me that I may do so. The infidel answered: I will sell it on condition that you encircle the island with colored clothing. The newcomer agreed with the infidel and bought on the condition stipulated. He encircled the island with clothing, some white, some black, and every other color besides. So the infidel agreed and took away all the clothing, handing over the island."

Some days later the African returned with his followers, intending to cross over to the island at low tide and attack the traders; but he found that the channel separating the island from the mainland had been deepened, making the crossing impassable. "Then he despaired of seizing the island and was sorry at what he had done. He went home full of remorse and sorrow."

As the largest of the southerly trading ports, Kilwa was able to obtain a monopoly of the trade in gold from the region of Zimbabwe, an inland kingdom to the south. The people of Zimbabwe were essentially cattle raisers, and the need to defend their large herds and distant grazing lands had led to the development of a centralized state under a royal dynasty. During the fourteenth century, the kings acquired new wealth from the export of gold that was mined from alluvial and reef deposits within their territory. The enormous walled enclosure known as Great Zimbabwe, constucted around the time when the gold trade was at its peak, was a vivid demonstration of the power and influence of the people of Zimbabwe.

Most of the gold was carried overland to Sofala, the nearest coastal settlement, from where it was shipped north to Kilwa. Once in Kilwa, heavy tariffs were levied on the bullion and on all other goods that passed through the port. The sultan's palace of Husuni Kubwa, containing more than 100 rooms, was said to be the largest building in Africa south of the Sahara. The indefatigable traveler ibn-Battuta, visiting the city of Kilwa in 1331, declared it to be "one of the most beautiful and well-constructed towns in the world."

The reasons why the Swahili culture and the influence of Islam did not penetrate farther inland were mainly geographic. Between the temperate grasslands and forests along the coast, watered by the monsoon rains, and the great lakes of the interior lay a wide belt of dry scrubland sparsely populated by tribes of warrior pastoralists who had neither the need nor the desire to alter their traditional patterns of life. Very few traders or foreigners ventured far from the coastal cities, although those who did were intrigued by what they found. A certain Chinese traveler, for example, gave a vivid account of two animals that were unfamiliar to him: One was "a kind of mule with brown, white, and black stripes around its body"; the other "resembles a camel in shape, an ox in size, and is of a yellow color. Its forelegs are five feet long, its hind legs only three feet. Its head is high up and turned upward." He was describing, of course, a zebra and a giraffe.

In the early decades of the fifteenth century, several expeditions from China arrived in the east-coast ports, whose prosperity continued unchecked. In 1415, a giraffe was sent from Malindi as a gift to the emperor of China, cementing this profitable partnership. But the exposed position of the trading cities and their lack of firm control over the hinterland were eventually to prove their undoing. They were discovered by the Portuguese navigator Vasco da Gama after he rounded the Cape of Good Hope in 1497; in the following decade, almost all the ports were sacked by Portuguese troops, and with them was destroyed the network of trade across the Indian Ocean. The coral palaces of the merchant rulers lay empty and in ruins.

Both Mali and the city-states of the east coast profited during the fourteenth century from trade and other friendly contacts with powerful Islamic countries in North Africa or across the Indian Ocean. These factors, however, were not indispensable in order to achieve prosperity. In the majestic mountains and on the sweltering plains of northern East Africa, inland from the coast of the Red Sea and the Horn of Africa, there flourished a kingdom that could hardly have been more different from Mali: It had no important trading ports, it was almost completely cut off from the outside world, and its religion was Christianity.

Christian doctrines had gained a firm foothold in Africa during the first centuries AD, when much of North Africa was governed by the Romans. How the religion arrived in the country that was to become known to outsiders as Ethiopia—from the word used in Greek texts of the Bible to describe the black peoples of Africa—was recounted by a chronicler named Rufinus shortly after the event occurred. A ship carrying a Syrian monk and his two young students home from India landed on the west coast of the Red Sea and met a hostile reception. After the monk and all the ship's crew had been killed, the two students, Aedisius and Frumentius, "were found studying under a tree and preparing their lessons." These evidently model children were taken as gifts to the king of the country. Aedisius became the king's cupbearer while Frumentius, whom the king perceived to be "sagacious and prudent," served

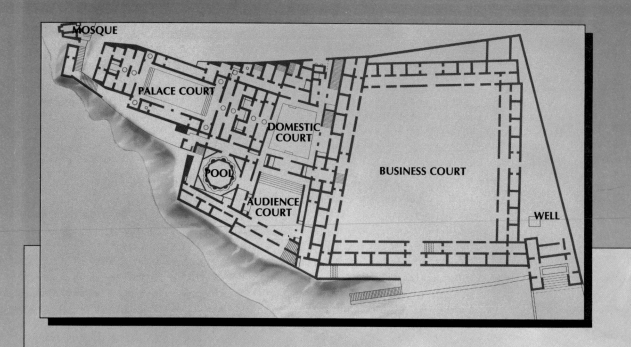

Constructed out of coral stone in the early fourteenth century, a sultan's palace dominates a cliff top on the island of Kilwa, just off the east coast of Africa. This edifice was the largest domestic residence in all of equatorial Africa. With more than 100 rooms, an octagonal bathing pool, and separate sections for residential and commercial purposes *(inset),* the palace advertised the ruler's wealth and power, which were based upon Kilwa's monopoly of the trade in gold transported from the interior.

Kilwa was one of the foremost of a string of more than thirty trading centers that thrived during the fourteenth century along the east coast of Africa. The distinctive Swahili culture of these mercantile centers emerged from a union of Bantu African and Muslim Arab influences. African goods arrived overland and in coastal vessels such as the one shown below; from Kilwa and the other ports, the merchandise was carried north to Arabia and east to India, Indonesia, and even as far as China.

as the royal secretary. After rising to high office, Frumentius was able to convert the king and his family to Christianity.

All this occurred around AD 350, and the kingdom in question was Aksum. The Aksumites wrote their language, Geez, in characters borrowed from the Sabeans of southern Arabia, with whom there had been strong trading and cultural links for many centuries. Out of this marriage of cultures came a rich and powerful state that survived into the ninth century, after which royal power moved south into the mountains of Ethiopia, at first to Lalibala and then, southward again, to the wild rifts and ranges of the kingdom of Shoa.

By this time, the other Christian states of Africa had succumbed to Islam. Christian Egypt had fallen to invading Arab armies in the seventh century, and in 1171, the Muslim lords of Egypt drove deeply southward into the Christian kingdoms of Nubia. But though sorely isolated from the rest of the Christian world by a ring of Muslim foes and rivals, the kingdom of Ethiopia became under the Solomonid dynasty a fortress of the faith that no aggression was able to overcome.

The dynasty was so named because its founder, King Yekuno-Amlak, who reigned from 1270 to 1285, claimed the dignity of descent from King Solomon of the Old Testament. How this came about was explained by the royal chronicler and also by wall paintings of the time, in graphic detail. The queen of Sheba (or Sabea) traveled to Jerusalem to visit Solomon, who admired her wealth and wisdom and her person even more. The chaste queen made Solomon promise not to take advantage of her and in return undertook not to take away any of his possessions. But after a great banquet including much wine and highly seasoned food, the queen woke in the night and drank water from a jar. Solomon, who had planned this event, accused her of taking what did not belong to her; the queen confessed her guilt and released Solomon from his promise. It was from their child, Menelik, that Yekuno-Amlak claimed direct descent.

The survival of Christian Ethiopia—or Abyssinia, as it was known to its own people—depended first of all on its ability to withstand attacks by neighboring Muslim powers. Abyssinia's army consisted mostly of foot soldiers armed with swords, iron-tipped lances, and short bows; horses were rare, and probably only the commanders possessed them. The lack of cavalry and armor notwithstanding, Ethiopian forces defeated four Muslim invasions in the first half of the fourteenth century. Their success was largely due to the leadership of King Amda Tseyon (Pillar of Zion), who rewarded his troops generously. "He took from his treasury," the chronicles recorded, "gold, silver, and garments of great beauty, which he distributed among his soldiers from the greatest to the least important: Because, in his reign, gold and silver abounded like stones, and fine garments were as numerous as the leaves on the trees or the grass in the fields."

Partly for military reasons and partly to gather tribute from local centers of population, the kings of Ethiopia moved from one temporary capital to another, living with their entourage in huge encampments that were abandoned when the surrounding pasture and wood for cooking fires had been exhausted. But in other ways, they ruled as traditional African kings, concealed from their subjects in palatial tents when not on the field of battle or holding court, and enveloped in pomp and mystery. Possible rivals for the throne were confined with their families on flat-topped hills to which precipitous cliffs gave only the most hazardous access; no one was allowed to climb up or down without the king's consent, a concession rarely granted.

Most of the peoples of the kingdom were small farmers and stock raisers. In many regions, the fertile soil yielded several crops a year; cotton and coffee were grown as well as wheat, barley, and a highly nutritious grain called teff, unique to Ethiopia. The farmers might possess their own land and cattle, but they had to pay taxes and tribute and perform obligatory labor service for the high-ranking warriors and clergy. Failure to carry out such duties and other serious offenses were punished by flogging, which was applied with merciless whips. But it could often happen—especially with offenders who had influence at court—that the whips struck the ground instead of the offender, the object being to instill fear in onlookers as well as the offender rather than to cause injury. Ethiopian society was based on small communities, and personal dignities were precious.

Culturally, the single most important factor in Ethiopia's national identity was the Church. Since the Council of Chalcedon in 451, the Christian churches in Africa had been separated from the Roman Catholic and Greek Orthodox churches in Europe by doctrinal differences, and when they ceased to use Greek after the Arab invasions in the seventh century, they had been further isolated by language barriers. The African Christians had become known as Copts—from the Arabic word for Egypt—and in the Muslim countries their numbers had dwindled. But in Ethiopia their faith had remained steadfast against the incursions of Islam, and the power of the Church was closely linked to that of the monarchy.

Continuing the tradition of patronage exemplified in the thirteenth century by King Lalibala, who had supervised the construction of a series of massive churches hewn out of solid rock near the town to which he gave his name, the Solomonid kings founded new monasteries and endowed the Church with vast holdings of land. In return, the church leaders actively supported the kings' wars against the Muslims and worked to convert the pagan tribes living in territory overrun by the army. The Ethiopian monks, the more ascetic members of the Church, produced fine manuscripts of chronicles, liturgical texts, and the lives of saints; they also maintained contact with their Coptic brethren in Egypt. Their extreme devoutness was personified by a fanatical monk named Eustathius, who mortified his flesh to prove his spiritual humility: He wrapped himself in iron chains that had been left in the sun until they were red-hot, so that his body resembled "a fish grilled in the fire."

The saints and holy men of the Church were celebrated in national legends that told of miraculous events. One such tale concerned Saint Abiya Egzi, who lived in the early fourteenth century: When the saint became lost while wandering in the wilderness, springs welled up to slake his thirst, wild animals approached to advise him, and an elephant guided him to a remote sanctuary. Another concerned a group of pilgrims who set out on a long and perilous journey and rested one night in a cave. The mouth of the cave became the mouth of a monstrous but kindly serpent that closed its jaws on the pilgrims and carried them safely to their destination.

Guided by the forceful successors of King Amda Tseyon, who died in 1344, Ethiopia continued to thrive throughout the fourteenth century. In 1352, when the patriarch of the Coptic church in Alexandria was imprisoned by the Mamluk sultanate of Egypt, King Saifa-Arad secured his release by threatening to execute or forcibly convert all Egyptian traders who ventured into Ethiopia; thereafter, relations between the two countries became increasingly friendly. Coptic texts in Arabic were translated into the Ethiopian liturgical language of Geez, and the church acquired from Jerusalem venerable holy relics including an alleged piece of the cross on which Christ was crucified. Tribute was exacted from some of the small independent Muslim states on the southern borders. And as Ethiopia's power and influence expanded, its isolation from the rest of the Christian world diminished.

Instrumental in the renewal of contacts with other Christian nations was the legend of Prester John. Since the time of the Crusades in the twelfth century, stories had circulated in Europe about a remote Christian ruler somewhere in the East. Believing this rumored sovereign to be a potential ally in their wars against Islam, European adventurers had sought for his kingdom in central Asia. But in 1306, a delegation of Ethiopians traveled to Europe and described to a Genoese cartographer, Giovanni da Carignano, their "most Christian emperor of Ethiopia," who owned the allegiance of seventy-four kings and of innumerable princes. From then on, the focus of the legend became Africa.

An increasing number of hardy European travelers, many of them motivated by the quest for Prester John, found their way into Ethiopia, where their skills were put to good use. One of them, a Venetian painter named Nicolo Brancaleone, resided in the kingdom for forty years in the fifteenth century, working on the decoration of churches; he was described by another visitor as "a very honorable person and a great gentleman, though a painter." In the early sixteenth century, Portuguese ships arrived in the Red Sea, and Ethiopia, beset by an invading Muslim army equipped with

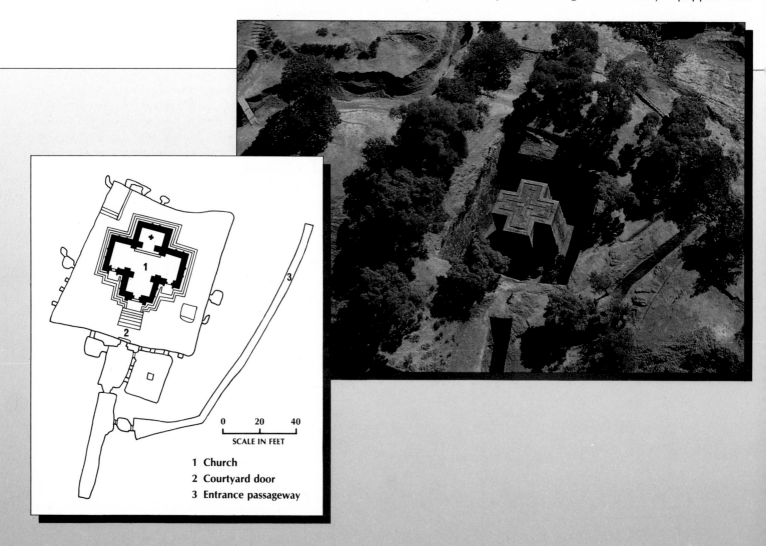

0   20   40
SCALE IN FEET

1 Church
2 Courtyard door
3 Entrance passageway

firearms and artillery, was saved from complete destruction only by the timely arrival of a force of Portuguese musketeers. By gradual stages, Ethiopia was thus drawn back into the worldwide Christian community, while maintaining the distinctive African traditions developed during its proud isolation.

For Europe and Asia in the fourteenth century, Africa south of the Sahara was represented by the gold, ivory, and slaves exported from Mali and the east-coast trading ports. Even the artifacts and monumental building works of the peoples of the interior remained largely unknown to the outside world: The rock churches of Ethiopia were first visited by Europeans toward the end of the fifteenth century, and the massive stone-built enclosure of Zimbabwe was not seen by Europeans until the latter part of the nineteenth century. Within this vast and unexplored continent, however, there existed peoples and cultures whose range and diversity made that portion of Africa known to the outside world seem like the tip of an iceberg. "The inhabitants of his country are numerous, a vast concourse," wrote the Arab scholar al-Umari of Mansa Musa's empire of Mali, "but compared to the peoples who are their neighbors and penetrate far to the south, they are like a white birthmark on a black cow."

Materially simple but culturally complex, the productive and organized lives of these people represented an achievement no less real than the opulent splendors of Mali or Ethiopia. They had mastered the problems of

In the rocky Ethiopian uplands of the Horn of Africa, the monolithic church of Saint George stands in an excavated pit forty feet deep. Tombs and monks' cells were cut into the side of the pit, and worshipers gained access to the church by following a sloping passage cut into the surrounding plain *(plan, far left)*.

Carved from solid rock in the shape of a cross and then hollowed out, this church was one of a group of ten in the vicinity that were constructed during the thirteenth century on the orders of King Lalibala, one of the most passionately devout of Ethiopia's Christian rulers.

Cavelike churches had been hewn out of the faces of cliffs in many places before, but freestanding buildings were an Ethiopian innovation. These churches were probably built with the assistance of Egyptian Coptic Christians fleeing persecution at the hands of the Muslims.

CHURCHES CARVED FROM LIVING ROCK

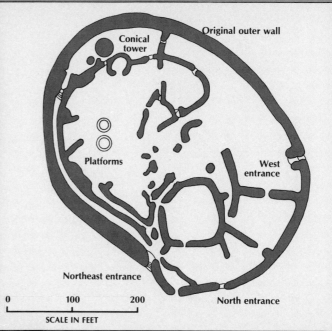

Conical
tower

Original outer wall

Platforms

West
entrance

Northeast entrance

North entrance

0   100   200

SCALE IN FEET

The majestic stone structures of Great Zimbabwe, constructed by the Shona people in the thirteenth and fourteenth centuries, were designed to dignify rather than to defend the largest city of southern Africa. Center of a cattle-raising economy that operated over great distances, the settlement lay on the rim of the central-southern plateau of Africa, between the dense scrubland of the winter pastures and the open country of the high veld.

The reconstruction at left shows a view within the Great Enclosure, which was probably the royal residence *(plan, above)*. A massive wall 820 feet long and more than thirty feet high, built of granite blocks without mortar, surrounded the thatched huts that belonged to the ruler's family as well as a number of ceremonial or symbolic structures; the latter included a conical tower and platforms for displaying carved artifacts and pots.

At intervals along the wall stood soapstone carvings; a number of these portrayed the sacred fish-eagle *(far left)*, the "Bird of Bright Plumage" revered by the 10,000 inhabitants of Great Zimbabwe as their guardian and counselor.

existence in every region of Africa—from the humid equatorial rain forests to the burning deserts of the south, from the mountainous eastern highlands to the grassy inland plateaus—and had developed strategies of survival and cooperation that were precisely attuned to their needs.

By the fourteenth century, settled agricultural societies—interspersed in regions less suitable for farming by seminomadic cattle-raising peoples—were thriving across the whole of Africa almost down to the Cape of Good Hope; the only exceptions to the farmers and herders were the Pygmies in the rain forests of the Congo and the Khoi of certain arid central and southern regions, who lived by hunting and gathering their food. The agricultural accomplishments of the African peoples had been made possible by two related developments during the first millennium AD. The first was the steady outward migration of Bantu-speaking peoples from their base in the lower Congo basin; these skilled ironworkers taught the societies they settled among how to make metal tools and so enabled them to penetrate densely populated terrain and to grow crops in previously uncultivated land. The second was the introduction of Southeast Asian foods—plantains, sugar, and new varieties of coconuts, rice, and yams—by Indonesian settlers in Madagascar; many of these foods could be grown in moist conditions and produced high yields.

Though linked to its neighbors by regional networks of trade, each community was largely self-sufficient and isolated; in relation to the vastness of their continent, the African people were few in number, and warfare for territorial gain was rare. As well as farming, many of the settled peoples mined for copper, tin, gold, or iron ore. The metals were used to make tools, weapons, and jewelry; wood, ivory, and terra cotta were also worked to make sculptures and other sacred objects.

The forms of social organization evolved by these peoples varied according to their size and the ecology of their territory, but certain features were shared by many. Each community generally comprised a number of lineage groups based on kinship and family descent, while farmers, artisans, and others with specialist occupations had fixed responsibilities and privileges according to the social value of their work. Blacksmiths in particular, who possessed the secrets of turning iron-bearing ores into useful metal, enjoyed a special status as almost magical beings. The seminomadic peoples were often divided by age: As they advanced in years, all the males of the same age became warriors and then elders at mass-initiation ceremonies.

Land was always collectively owned, and wealth was measured not in territory but often in the number of animals that a person owned. In the more centralized societies, the power of the king was perceived as the accumulated wisdom and strength handed down by the ancestors, and the health of the king was intimately associated with that of the community as a whole.

Underpinning the social framework was African religion. Centuries older than Islam and Christianity, African systems of belief posited a world of ancestral and natural spirits whose influence upon daily life could be beneficial or harmful. The supernatural was experienced as natural: Good fortune in war or the growth of crops could be invoked by ritual ceremonies, and wrongdoing would be punished by witchcraft. The dignity and meaning of individual lives lay in their relationship to the community, which consisted of the dead and the still-to-be-born as well as the living. Such beliefs functioned as unwritten codes of justice: They sanctified custom and authority and embodied clear ideals of behavior.

Through the rhythms of their music and dancing, through their shrines and sacred precincts, through the masks and sculptures made by anonymous artisans, the Africans linked themselves to their ancestors and to a spirit world that existed parallel to, and sometimes infringing upon, their own. Such beliefs and practices gave stability and a firm sense of identity to the local communities and hallowed their relationship with the land that sustained them.

Because they did not constitute a set of fixed doctrines but provided an infinitely flexible means of interpreting their experience, the religious beliefs of the Africans enabled them to absorb many external influences without undue disruption. Large-scale migrations, the acquisition of new skills such as ironworking, and the generation of new political ideas were all of momentous consequence, but each of these was subsumed into what was essentially a continuous, unbroken course of development and achievement.

Throughout the fourteenth century, even the activities of foreign travelers, merchants, and scholars in the kingdoms of the Sudan and the city-states on the east coast did not alienate these societies from their longstanding cultural traditions. Islam brought literacy and the stimulus of its own scholarly traditions; it introduced new political ideas and commercial practices; and it drew large parts of Africa into the international trading network that linked all the countries of Europe and Asia. But these benefits were accepted and exploited by the Africans without compromising their own cultural identity.

Contacts between the peoples of sub-Saharan Africa and incomers from other cultures were never again to be so fruitful. As the nations of Europe became dependent on supplies of African gold to sustain their economies, they began to contemplate the advantages of controlling its production as well as its consumption. By the end of the sixteenth century, during which ships from Europe traversed the globe, the nations to the north would attain the power to do so. They would also—in their need for labor to work the mines and plantations of their American colonies—acquire another motive for intruding on the African kingdoms. The intricately balanced structures of African societies, the product of milleniums of gradual evolution, were to be violently disrupted by the arrival of the Europeans. ▬

1300-1310	1310-1320	1320-1330	1330-1340	1340-1350

WESTERN EUROPE

1330-1340: Yusuf I, the Moorish ruler of Granada, extends and embellishes the Alhambra.

Edward III of England defeats the Scots and occupies the south of Scotland (1336); the deposed son of Robert Bruce is given shelter in France.

Edward III refuses to pay homage to Philip VI for English territory in France (1337), thus precipitating the Hundred Years' War.

1300-1310: Edward I dies; Edward II succeeds to the English throne (1307).

The papal court is moved from Rome to Avignon (1309), where it comes under French political influence.

1310-1320: Scotland confirms independence from England with Robert Bruce's victory over Edward II at Bannockburn (1314).

The Italian poet Dante starts writing *The Divine Comedy* (1314).

1320-1330: Edward II of England is deposed and succeeded by his son Edward III (1327).

Following the death of Charles IV of France, his nephew Philip VI founds the Valois dynasty (1328).

1340-1350: The French navy is defea[ted by] the English at Sluis (134[0]).

English armies win the B[attle of] Crécy (1346) and captur[e the] port of Calais (1347).

The Black Death reaches [Europe] from Asia (1347) and cla[ims] million lives in the follow[ing] four years.

THE MIDDLE EAST AND CENTRAL ASIA

1300-1310: Under their leader Osman, the Ottoman tribal warriors of northeast Anatolia win their first engagement against an army of the Byzantine Empire (1301).

The empire of the Seljuks in southeast Anatolia begins to fall apart.

1320-1330: The Ottomans capture the Byzantine city of Bursa in Anatolia and make it their capital (1326).

Orhan succeeds his father, Osman, as Ottoman ruler and takes the title of sultan (1326).

1330-1340: Stephen Dushan accedes to the throne of Serbia (1331) and begins to create a Serbian empire in the Balkans.

Orhan seizes the Byzantine towns of Nicaea (1331) and Nicomedia (1337) and extends the Ottoman frontier to the Sea of Marmara.

1340-1350: Ottoman troops enter ea[stern] Europe to aid the Byzant[ine em]peror Cantacuzene, who [gives] his daughter in marriage [to Or]han (1346).

CHINA

1310-1320: The Mongol emperor Ayurbarwada reintroduces civil-service examinations based on Confucian texts (1315).

1320-1330: Zhu Yuanzhang, future founder of the Ming dynasty, is born to a family of peasant farmers (1328).

Floods, famine, and epidemics cause widespread loss of life throughout China.

1330-1340: Popular rebellions in central and southern China, incited by the harsh measures of the Mongol chancellor Bayan, are ruthlessly suppressed.

The White Lotus and other secret societies begin to foster revolt against the Yuan dynasty of the Mongols.

1340-1350: Bayan is overthrown in a [coup] and dies (1340). Rebel ar[mies] known as the Red Turban[s win] widespread support in the [lower] Yangtze and Huai valleys.

The Mongol chancellor T[oghto] initiates a dynamic progra[m to] clear the blocked Grand [Canal] and restore Mongol contr[ol] (1349).

AFRICA

1310-1320: Mansa Musa becomes ruler of Mali (1312) and encourages Islamic cultural and commercial practices.

Amda Tseyon, the grandson of the founder of the Solomonic dynasty, becomes king of Ethiopia (1314).

1320-1330: Amda Tseyon wages war on Muslim kingdoms bordering on Christian Ethiopia.

Mansa Musa of Mali makes a pilgrimage to Mecca via Cairo (1324).

1330-1340: The Arab traveler ibn-Battuta visits the wealthy city-states of the east coast (1331).

Mansa Musa, emperor of Mali, dies (1337) and is eventually succeeded by his brother Mansa Suleyman.

1340-1350: Amda Tseyon of Ethiopia [dies] and is succeeded by Saifa[Arad] (1344).

TimeFrame: AD 1300-1400

1360	1360-1370	1370-1380	1380-1390	1390-1400
...k Prince, son of Edward ... the Battle of Poitiers ...tures the French king, ...356). ...querie, a peasant rebel- ...rance, is suppressed by ...ohn (1358).	A nine-year truce between England and France follows the Treaty of Brétigny (1360). John II of France dies in captivity and is succeeded by Charles V (1364). The Italian poet Petrarch publishes his *Canzoniere* (1366). France renews the war against England (1369) and begins to reconquer territory ceded to England at Brétigny.	The English navy is defeated by the French and Castilian fleets at La Rochelle (1372). Richard II succeeds Edward III as king of England (1377). After the return of the papal court to Rome in 1377 and the election of Urban VI, the Great Schism begins when a rebellious group of cardinals elect Clement VII, who takes up residence in Avignon (1378). The Venetians defeat their merchant rivals the Genoese at the War of Chioggia (1380).	Charles VI succeeds Charles V as king of France (1380). The Peasants' Revolt in England is suppressed and its leader, Wat Tyler, executed (1381). Portugal secures independence after defeating Castile at Aljubarrota (1385). The English poet Chaucer writes the *Canterbury Tales* (1388). England and France commence peace negotiations at Leulinghen in France (1389).	Richard II of England marries Isabella, daughter of Charles VI of France (1396). Richard II is deposed by Henry Bolingbroke, who succeeds as Henry IV (1399).
...omans seize the fortress ...poli on the west bank of ...danelles (1354). ...Dushan dies (1355) and ...ian empire begins to ...rate.	Murad I succeeds Orhan as Ottoman ruler and captures Adrianople (1361); the city is renamed Edirne and becomes the Ottoman base in eastern Europe. The renowned Persian poet Hafiz writes his *Divan* (1368). Tamerlane becomes master of the Chagatai khanate of Transoxiana (1369). John Palaeologus, emperor of Byzantium, declares his allegiance to the Catholic church in Rome (1369).	The Ottomans defeat the Serbians and Hungarians at Maritza (1371) and begin to occupy Balkan territory. From his base at Samarkand, Tamerlane campaigns against the neighboring regions of Moghulistan and Khorasan.	Tamerlane invades Persia (1381) and Afghanistan; rebellions in Persian cities are brutally suppressed. The Balkan cities of Bitolj (1380), Sofia (1385), Nis (1386), and Salonika (1387) fall to the Ottomans. Murad I defeats the Serbians at Kosovo but is assassinated on the battlefield (1389).	Tamerlane sacks Sarai, capital of the Russian empire of the Golden Horde (1395). The Ottoman sultan Bajazet I annexes principalities in Anatolia, defeats an army of European Crusaders and Hungarians at Nicopolis on the Danube (1396), and blockades Constantinople. Tamerlane invades India and sacks Delhi (1398).
...s dismissed from office ...nd rebellion spreads ...ut China. ...l leader Zhu Yuanzhang ...anking (1355); three ...bel bases are established ...Yangtze.	Zhu defeats the forces of Chen Youliang, a rival leader, in a naval battle on Lake Poyang (1363). Zhu proclaims the new dynasty of the Ming—"Brilliant"—(1368); henceforth, he is known by his reign title as the Hongwu emperor. The Mongol capital of Dadu surrenders and the last Yuan emperor flees to Mongolia.	The Ming commander Xu Da invades Mongolia (1372). The Hongwu emperor initiates programs to repopulate devastated regions of northern China and stimulate agriculture.	The emperor orders the execution of his chancellor, Hu Weiyong, whom he suspects of plotting against him (1380); more than 30,000 officials are killed in subsequent purges. The office of chancellor is abolished and the emperor assumes direct personal control of the government.	Many thousands are executed in purges following the trial of a general accused of treason (1393). The Hongwu emperor dies (1398) and is succeeded by his grandson.
...uta visits Mali (1352- ...nd praises its just and ... government.	Mansa Suleyman of Mali dies (1360) and his empire begins to decline.		David I becomes king of Ethiopia (1382); during his reign, a number of contacts are made with Christian nations outside Africa.	

BIBLIOGRAPHY

BOOKS (GENERAL)

The Arts of Islam. London: Arts Council of Great Britain, 1976.

Atil, Esin, *Art of the Arab World.* Washington, D.C.: Smithsonian Institution, 1975.

Berrall, Julia S., *The Garden.* London: Thames and Hudson, 1966.

Bourne, Jonathan, et al., *Lacquer: An International History and Collector's Guide.* Marlborough, Wiltshire: The Crowood Press, 1984.

Burke, James, *The Day the Universe Changed.* London: BBC Publications, 1985.

Goode, Patrick, and Michael Lancaster, *The Oxford Companion to Gardens.* Oxford: Oxford University Press, 1986.

Gothein, Marie Luise, *History of Garden Art.* New York: Hacker Art Books, 1966.

Lewis, Bernard, ed., *The World of Islam.* London: Thames and Hudson, 1976.

McNeill, William H., *Plagues and Peoples.* Oxford: Basil Blackwell, 1977.

Michell, George, ed., *Architecture of the Islamic World.* London: Thames and Hudson, 1978.

Rice, David Talbot, *Islamic Art.* London: Thames and Hudson, 1975.

Rogers, Michael, *The Spread of Islam.* Oxford: Elsevier-Phaidon, 1976.

WESTERN EUROPE

Aldis, Elijah, *Carvings and Sculptures of Worcester Cathedral.* London: Bemrose and Sons, 1873.

Alexander, Jonathan, and Paul Binski, eds., *Age of Chivalry: Art in Plantagenet England, 1200-1400.* London: Royal Academy of Arts and Weidenfeld and Nicolson, 1987.

Allmand, C., ed., *Society at War.* Edinburgh: Oliver and Boyd, 1973.

Barber, R. W., *The Knight and Chivalry.* London: Boydell, 1970.

Barnie, J., *War in Medieval Society.* London: Weidenfeld and Nicolson, 1974.

Barraclough, Geoffrey, *The Medieval Papacy.* London: Thames and Hudson, 1968.

Blackmore, H. L., *The Armouries of the Tower of London.* London: Her Majesty's Stationery Office, 1976.

Bond, Francis, *Wood Carvings in English Churches.* London: Oxford University Press, 1910.

Contamine, Philippe, *War in the Middle Ages.* Transl. by Michael Jones. Oxford: Basil Blackwell, 1984.

Duby, Georges, *History of Medieval Art, 980-1440.* London: Skira / Weidenfeld and Nicolson, 1986.

Dupuy, R. Ernest, and Trevor N. Dupuy, *The Encyclopedia of Military History.* London: Military Book Society, 1970.

Evans, Joan, ed., *The Flowering of the Middle Ages.* London: Thames and Hudson, 1966.

Fossier, Robert, *Le Moyen Age.* Paris: Armand Colin, 1983.

Fowler, K.:
The Age of Plantagenet and Valois. London: Elek, 1967.
The Hundred Years' War. London: Macmillan, 1971.

Froissart, Jean, *Chronicles.* Transl. by Geoffrey Brereton. Harmondsworth, England: Penguin Books, 1987.

Gimpel, Jean, *The Medieval Machine.* London: Victor Gollancz, 1977.

Given-Wilson, C., ''War, Politics and Parliament,'' in *The Making of Britain.* Ed. by Lesley M. Smith. London: Macmillan, 1985.

Grabar, Oleg, *The Alhambra.* London: Allen Lane, 1978.

Hamel, Christopher de, *A History of Illuminated Manuscripts.* Oxford: Phaidon, 1986.

Hartley, Dorothy, and Margaret M. Elliot, *Life and Work of the People of England.* London: B. T. Batsford, 1928.

Harvey, John, *Mediaeval Gardens.* London: B. T. Batsford, 1981.

Hennebo, Dieter, *Gäarten des Mittelalters.* Munich: Artemis Verlag, 1987.

Hime, Henry W. L., *The Origin of Artillery.* London: Longmans, Green and Co., 1915.

Jean de Venette, *The Chronicles of Jean de Venette.* Transl. by J. Birdsall, ed. by R. Newhall. New York: Columbia University Press, 1953.

Keen, M., *The Laws of War in the Late Middle Ages.* London: Routledge and Kegan Paul, 1965.

Larner, John, *Culture and Society in Italy, 1290-1420.* London: B. T. Batsford, 1971.

Loomis, Roger Sherman, *A Mirror of Chaucer's World.* Princeton, New Jersey: Princeton University Press, 1966.

McEvedy, Colin, ''The Bubonic Plague.'' *Scientific American,* February 1988.

McFarlane, K. B., ''England and the Hundred Years' War,'' Vol. 22, *Past and Present.* London, 1962.

Mollat, M., and P. Wolff, *The Popular Revolutions of the Late Middle Ages.* London: George Allen and Unwin, 1973.

Palmer, John Joseph Norman, *England, France and Christendom, 1377-1399.* London: Routledge and Kegan Paul, 1972.

Postan, M. M., ''The Costs of the Hundred Years' War,'' Vol. 27, *Past and Present.* London, 1964.

Prestwich, Michael, *The Three Edwards: War and State in England, 1272-1377.* London: Methuen, 1981.

Reid, William, *Weapons through the Ages.* London: Peerage Books, 1984.

Remnant, G. L., *A Catalogue of Misericords in Great Britain.* Oxford: Oxford University Press, 1969.

Rogers, H. C. B., *Artillery through the Ages.* London: Seeley Service & Co., 1972.

Rothero, Christopher, *The Armies of Crécy and Poitiers.* London: Osprey Publishing, 1981.

Strutt, Joseph, *The Sports and Pastimes of the People of England.* London: William Reeves, 1830.

Thomas, Keith, *Religion and the Decline of Magic.* Harmondsworth, England: Penguin Books, 1982.

Tuchman, Barbara W., *A Distant Mirror.* London: Macmillan, 1978.

White, Henry W. L., *The Origin of Artillery.* London: Longmans, Green and Co., 1915.

Ziegler, Philip, *The Black Death.* London: Penguin Books, 1982.

THE OTTOMAN WORLD

Atiya, Aziz Suryal, *The Crusade in the Later Middle Ages.* London: Methuen, 1938.

Bodur, Fulya, *Türk Maden Sanati: The Art of Turkish Metalworking.* Istanbul: Türk Kültürüne Hizmet Vakfi Sanat Yayinlari, 1987.

Eversley, Lord, *The Turkish Empire from 1288 to 1914.* New York: Howard Fertig, 1969.

Gibbons, Herbert Adams, *The Foundation of the Ottoman Empire.* Oxford: Clarendon Press, 1916.

Goodwin, Godfrey, *A History of Ottoman Architecture.* London: Thames and Hudson, 1971.

Hetherington, Paul, *Byzantium: City of Gold, City of Faith.* London: Orbis Publishing, 1983.

Holt, P. M., Ann K. S. Lambton, and Bernard Lewis, *The Cambridge History of Islam.* Vol. 1. Cambridge: Cambridge University Press, 1970.

Inalcik, Halil, *The Ottoman Empire.* Transl. by Norman Itzkowitz and Colin Imber. London: Weidenfeld and Nicolson, 1973.

Ipsiroglu, Mazhar S., *Masterpieces from the Topkapi Museum: Paintings and Miniatures.* London: Thames and Hudson, 1980.

Kinross, Lord, *The Ottoman Centuries.* London: Jonathan Cape, 1977.

Nicol, Donald M., *The Last Centuries of Byzantium.* London: Rupert Hart-Davis, 1972.

Nicolle, D., *Armies of the Ottoman Turks, 1300-1774.* London: Osprey Publishing, 1983.

Parry, V. J., and M. E. Yapp, eds., *War, Technology and Society in the Middle East.* London: Oxford University Press, 1975.

Petsopoulos, Yanni, ed., *Tulips, Arabesques & Turbans: Decorative Arts from the Ottoman Empire.* London: Alexandria Press, 1982.

Runciman, S., *A History of the Crusades.* Vol. 3. Harmondsworth, England: Penguin Books, 1954.

Shaw, Stanford J., *History of the Ottoman Empire and Modern Turkey.* Vol. 1. Cambridge: Cambridge University Press, 1976.

Smith, G. Rex, *Medieval Muslim Horsemanship.* London: The British Library, 1979.

TAMERLANE'S EMPIRE

Andrews, Peter Alford, "The Felt Tent in Middle Asia: The Nomadic Tradition and Its Interaction with Princely Tentage." Unpublished Ph.D. thesis, University of London, 1980.

Ibn Arabshah, Ahmed, *Tamerlane, or Timur the Great Amir.* Transl. by J. H. Sanders. London: Luzac & Co., 1936.

Aubin, Jean, "Comment Tamerlan Prenait les Villes." *Studia Islamica,* 19, 1963.

Bertrando de Mignanelli, "Vita Tamerlani. A New Latin Source on Tamerlane's Conquest." Ed. and transl. by W. J. Fischel. *Oriens,* 9, 1956.

Borodina, Iraida, *Central Asia.* Moscow: Planeta Publishers, 1987.

Brent, Peter, *The Mongol Empire.* London: Weidenfeld and Nicolson, 1976.

Browne, Edward Granville, *A Literary History of Persia.* Vol. 3. Cambridge: Cambridge University Press, 1928.

Clavijo, Ruy González de, *Embassy to Tamerlane (1403-1406).* Transl. by G. le Strange. London: Broadway, 1928.

Golombek, Lisa, and Donald Wilber, *The Timurid Architecture of Iran and Turan.* Vol. 2. Princeton, New Jersey: Princeton University Press, 1988.

Gray, Basil, *Persian Painting.* London: Skira / Macmillan, 1977.

Grube, E. J., "Notes on the Decorative Arts of the Timurid Period," in *Gururajamanjarika: Studi in Onore di Giuseppe Tucci.* Vol 1. Naples: Istituto Universitario Orientale, 1974.

Hodgson, Marshal G. S., *The Venture of Islam.* Vol. 2. Chicago: Chicago University Press, 1974.

Hookham, Hilda, *Tamburlaine the Conqueror.* London: Hodder and Stoughton, 1962.

Ipsiroglu, Mazhar S., *Painting and Culture of the Mongols.* Transl. by E. D. Phillips. London: Thames and Hudson, 1967.

Jackson, Peter, and Laurence Lockhart, eds., *The Cambridge History of Iran.* Vol. 6. Cambridge: Cambridge University Press, 1986.

John of Sultaniyya, "Mémoire sur Tamerlan et Sa Cour par un Dominicain en 1403." Transl. by H. Moranvillé. *Bibliothèque de l'École des Chartes,* 55, 1894.

Ibn Khaldun, *Ibn Khaldun and Tamerlane: Their Historic Meeting in Damascus, 1401,* from Ibn Khaldun's Autobiography. Transl. by W. J. Fischel. Berkeley, California: University of California Press, 1952.

Lamb, Harold, *Tamerlane: The Earth Shaker.* London: Thornton Butterworth, 1949.

Manz, Beatrice Forbes, "The Ulus Chagatay before and after Temur's Rise to Power." *Central Asiatic Journal,* 27, 1983.

Morgan, David, *Medieval Persia, 1040-1797.* London: Longmans, 1988.

Robinson, B. W., *Persian Miniature Painting.* London: Her Majesty's Stationery Office, 1967.

Ibn Taghribirdi, *History of Egypt from Arabic Annals of Abul Mahasin ibn Taghri Birdi (1382-1469).* Transl. by W. Popper. Berkeley, California: University of California Press, 1954.

Titley, Norah M., *Persian Miniature Painting.* London: The British Library, 1983.

CHINA

Cahill, James, *Hills beyond a River: Chinese Painting of the Yüan Dynasty, 1279-1368.* New York: John Weatherhill Inc., 1976.

Cammann, Schuyler, *China's Dragon Robes.* New York: The Ronald Press Co., 1952.

Dardess, J. W.:
Confucianism and Autocracy. Berkeley, California: University of California Press, 1983.
Conquerors and Confucians. New York: Columbia University Press, 1973.

Dreyer, E. L., *Early Ming China: A Political History.* Stanford, California: Stanford University Press, 1982.

Elvin, M., *The Pattern of the Chinese Past.* London: Eyre Methuen, 1973.

Farmer, E. L.:
Early Ming Government. Cambridge, Massachusetts: Harvard University Press, 1976.
Gardens in Chinese Art. New York: China House Gallery, 1968.

Gernet, Jacques, *A History of Chinese Civilization.* Transl. by J. R. Foster. Cambridge: Cambridge University Press, 1982.

Goodrich, L. Carrington, and Chaoying Fang, eds., *Dictionary of Ming Biography.* Vols. 1 and 2. New York: Columbia University Press, 1976.

The Horizon Book of the Arts of China. New York: American Heritage Publishing Co., 1969.

Hsiao, C. C., *The Military Establishment of the Yuan Dynasty.* Cambridge, Massachusetts: Harvard University Press, 1978.

Hucker, C. O., *China's Imperial Past.* Stanford, California: Stanford University Press, 1975.

Hucker, C. O., ed., *Chinese Government in Ming Times.* New York: Columbia University Press, 1981.

Keswick, Maggie, *The Chinese Garden.* London: Academy Editions, 1978.

Langlois, J. D., ed., *China under Mongol Rule.* Princeton, New Jersey: Princeton University Press, 1981.

Lawton, Thomas, *Chinese Figure Painting.* Washington, D.C.: David Godine / Freer Gallery of Art, Smithsonian Institution, 1973.

Lion-Goldschmidt, Daisy, *Ming Porcelain.* Transl. by Katherine Watson. London: Thames and Hudson, 1978.

Morris, Edwin T., *The Gardens of China.* New York: Charles Scribner's Sons, 1983.

Mote, Frederick W., and Denis Twitchett, eds., *The Cambridge History of China.* Vol. 7. Cambridge: Cambridge University Press, 1988.

Needham, Joseph, *Science and Civilisation in China.* Vol. 4, Part 3. Cambridge: Cambridge University Press, 1971.

Rawson, Jessica, *Chinese Ornament: The Lotus and the Dragon.* London: British Museums Publications Ltd., 1984.

Sirén, Osvald, *Gardens of China.* New York: The Ronald Press Company, 1949.

Swann, Peter C., *Art of China, Korea and Japan.* London: Thames and Hudson, 1963.

Waldron, Arthur, "The Problem of the Great Wall." *Harvard Journal of Asiatic Studies,* Vol. 43, No. 2, December 1983.

AFRICA

Buxton, David, *The Abyssinians.* London: Thames and Hudson, 1970.

Chittick, Neville, *Kilwa: An Islamic Trading City on the East African Coast.* Vols. 1 and 2. Nairobi: The British Institute in Eastern Africa, 1974.

Davidson, Basil, *Africa in History.* London: Paladin / Grafton Books, 1984.

Davidson, Basil, and the Editors of Time-Life Books, *African Kingdoms* (The Great Ages of Man series). Amsterdam: Time-Life Books, 1966.

Doresse, Jean, *Ethiopia.* London: Elek, 1959.

Eyo, Ekpo, and Frank Willett, *Treasures of Ancient Nigeria.* New York: Alfred A. Knopf, 1980.

Fage, J. D., *A History of Africa.* London: Hutchinson, 1978.

Freeman-Grenville, G. S. P., *The East African Coast: Select Documents from the First to the Earlier Nineteenth Century.* Oxford: Clarendon Press, 1962.

Garlake, Peter S.:
The Early Islamic Architecture of the East African Coast. Nairobi: Oxford University Press, 1966.
Great Zimbabwe. London: Thames and Hudson, 1973.
Great Zimbabwe Described and Explained. Harare, Zimbabwe: Zimbabwe Publishing House, 1982.
Life at Great Zimbabwe. Zimbabwe: Mambo Press, 1982.

Hopkins, J. F. P., transl., *Corpus of Early Arabic Sources for West African History.* Cambridge: Cambridge University Press, 1981.

Oliver, Roland, and J. D. Fage, *A Short History of Africa.* London: Penguin Books, 1988.

Pankhurst, Richard, *An Introduction to the Economic History of Ethiopia.* Woodford Green, Essex, England: Lalibela House, 1961.

Pankhurst, Sylvia, *Ethiopia: A Cultural History.* Woodford Green, Essex, England: Lalibela House, 1955.

Prins, H. J., *Sailing from Lamu.* Assen, the Netherlands: Van Gorcum and Comp. N. V. Dr. H. J. Prakke & H. M. G. Prakke, 1965.

Trimingham, J. Spencer, *The Influence of Islam upon Africa.* London: Longman, 1980.

Willett, Frank, *Ife in the History of West African Sculpture.* London: Thames and Hudson, 1967.

PICTURE CREDITS

ACKNOWLEDGMENTS

The following materials have been reprinted with the kind permission of the publishers: Page 32: "No cock crowed . . ." and "In truth, the more money . . .," quoted in *The Chronicles of Jean de Venette*, ed. by R. Newhall, New York: Columbia University Press, 1953. Page 35: "numerous crimes and extortions . . .," quoted in "War, Politics and Parliament," in *The Making of Britain*, by C. Given-Wilson, ed. by Lesley M. Smith, London: Macmillan, 1985. Page 52: "fine and populous city . . ." and "the greatest of the Turkmen Kings . . .," quoted in *The Ottoman Centuries: The Rise and Fall of the Turkish Empire*, by Lord Kinross, London: Jonathan Cape, 1977. Page 64: "The tyrant thought . . .," quoted in *The Last Centuries of Byzantium*, by D. M. Nicol, London: Rupert Hart-Davies, 1972. Page 92: "This king Timur . . .," quoted in *Ibn Khaldun and Tamerlane: Their Historic Meeting in Damascus, 1401*, from Ibn Khaldun's Autobiography, transl. by W. J. Fischel, Berkeley and Los Angeles: University of California Press, 1952. Chapter 4: Quotations from Ming emperor taken from *Confucianism and Autocracy*, by J. W. Dardess, Berkeley: University of California Press, 1983. Chapter 5: Quotations from Arab historians al-Umari, al-Bakri, and ibn-Battuta taken from *Corpus of Early Arabic Sources for West African History*, transl. by J. F. P. Hopkins, Cambridge: Cambridge University Press, 1981.

The editors also wish to thank the following individuals and institutions for their valuable assistance in the preparation of this volume:
England: Cambridge—John Hatcher, Reader in Economic and Social History, University of Cambridge. Frome, Somerset—Dr. John H. Harvey. London—Janet Backhouse, Curator of Illuminated Manuscripts, British Library; Elizabeth Baquedano; John Cayley, Oriental Collections, British Library; Lesley Coleman; Jeremy Davies; Julia Engelhardt; Anne Farrer, Department of Oriental Antiquities, British Museum; Timothy Fraser; Mary Jane Gibson; Godfrey Goodwin, Royal Asiatic Society; Victor Harris, Department of Oriental Antiquities, British Museum; Gillian Hutchinson, National Maritime Museum; Angus Konstam, The Royal Armouries, H.M. Tower of London; Jane Portal, Department of Oriental Antiquities, British Museum; Julian Raby; Thom Richardson, Senior Curator of Armour, The Royal Armouries, H.M. Tower of London; B. W. Robinson; Rosemary Scott, Percival David Foundation; Brian A. Tremain, Photographic Service, British Museum; Linda Woolley, Department of Textile Furnishings and Dress, Victoria and Albert Museum; Jan Woudstra; Yoshiko Yasumura, School of Oriental and African Studies. Oxford—William Leaf; Linda Proud; Luke Treadwell. York—Peter H. Goodchild, Centre for the Conservation of Historic Parks and Gardens, IoAAS, University of York.
France: Paris—François Avril, Curateur, Département des Manuscrits, Bibliothèque Nationale; Béatrice Coti, Directrice du Service Iconographique, Éditions Mazenod; Antoinette Decaudin, Documentaliste, Département des Antiquités Orientales, Musée du Louvre; Michel Fleury, Président de la IV Section de l'École Pratique des Hautes Études; Marie Montembault, Documentaliste, Département des Antiquités Grecques et Romaines, Musée du Louvre.
Italy: Milan—Monsignor Enrico Galbiati, Biblioteca Ambrosiana.
Scotland: Edinburgh—Robert Hillenbrand.
Turkey: Istanbul—Ara Güler.
USA: California—Thomas Lentz, Los Angeles County Museum of Art. New York—Eleanor Sims.

INDEX